THE

NAKED

SALESPERSON

THE NAKED SALESPERSON

A **STRIPPED DOWN** APPROACH TO SELLING WITH **CONFIDENCE**

RENÉE WALKUP,
FOUNDER AND PRESIDENT OF SALESPEAK, INC.®
AND SANDRA MCKEE

A BUSINESS

Avon, Massachusetts

Published by
Adams Business, an imprint of Adams Media,
a division of F+W Media, Inc.
57 Littlefield Street, Avon, MA 02322. U.S.A.
www.adamsmedia.com

ISBN 10: 1-59869-852-4
ISBN 13: 978-1-59869-852-7

Printed in the United States of America.

10 9 8 7 6 5 4 3 2 1

Library of Congress Cataloging-in-Publication Data
is available from the publisher.

This publication is designed to provide accurate and authoritative
information with regard to the subject matter covered. It is sold with
the understanding that the publisher is not engaged in rendering legal,
accounting, or other professional advice. If legal advice or other expert
assistance is required, the services of a competent professional person
should be sought.
—From a *Declaration of Principles* jointly adopted by a Committee of
the American Bar Association and a Committee of Publishers and
Associations

Many of the designations used by manufacturers and sellers to distin-
guish their product are claimed as trademarks. Where those designations appear in this book and Adams Media was aware of a trademark
claim, the designations have been printed with initial capital letters.

This book is available at quantity discounts for bulk purchases.
For information, please call 1-800-289-0963.

The authors dedicate this book to all sales professionals whose success has suffered due to a fear of presenting. Our wish is that you will find new enthusiasm for your work and new rewards for your sales efforts.

Acknowledgments

Sandra McKee would like to acknowledge the brilliance, unflagging enthusiasm, (and occasional nagging) of coauthor Renée Walkup during the development of this book. She also thanks clients and students who have affirmed, by their progress and feedback, the methods that appear in this book. In addition, Amanda and Sandy Stahl have provided both emotional support and no-holds-barred reality checks on the usefulness of the content throughout the process.

And speaking of nagging, Renée Walkup would like to thank Sandra McKee for helping to make this book a reality. Sandra, you are an inspiration and you never fail to impress me with your skills as a talented writer and storyteller. I would also like to thank my hundreds of clients for their trust and support over these last thirteen years since founding SalesPEAK. You are the people who charge me up in the morning and throughout every day.

Lastly, to my husband, Ted, for all you do to support me in my work, and my daughter, Rachel, for your patience with my time spent on this project, thank you both!

Both Renée and Sandra thank Paula Munier, Director of Product Development at Adams Media, for her enthusiasm for our project from that first meeting in Boston. Brendan O'Neill also receives our appreciation as the one who kept on top of what was due and contributed his editorial expertise. We also want to acknowledge the production and layout staff for the professional and engaging appearance of the final product.

CONTENTS

Chapter 7
TAKING YOUR PITCH ABROAD 159

Chapter 8
PERFECT THE
FOLLOW-THROUGH 181

Introduction

When networking, we all know that when you introduce two people you should include some reason why the two will enjoy talking, as it is an excellent approach to building a connection between them. That way, after you leave, those people will have a basis for conversation.

It might go something like this:

> Jordan, I'd like you to meet Brett Dunbar. Brett, this is Jordan Smith. Jordan owns a car dealership that specializes in high-end vehicles. Jordan, Brett owns an exotic car rental agency.

Those two would likely be able to begin a conversation and possibly even find a way to help each other.

Introducing a sales presentation skills book to you, the reader, presents a bit more of a challenge.

> Rachel, I'd like to acquaint you with a book about a process that most people equate to having a root canal. *The Naked Salesperson*, meet Rachel who is missing sales opportunities because she sweats and freaks out at even the *thought* of making a presentation to a group.

As you can see, there is a bit of a challenge here. Look at it this way, though. You have ideas, great ideas. They might even be worth a fortune—either for your own dreams or for the company you represent. But the thought of pitching those ideas in a roomful of people shuts you down completely. Or, you may find that you ramble endlessly, without focus and direction. For this reason, you've seriously limited your chances of "landing the big one" because "big one" decisions are often made by more than one person, which puts you back into the whole roomful scenario.

As sales practitioners and professional speakers as well as authors on the subject, we could try to explain this book and the power its skills can bring to you. But, we thought it better to let an outside party familiar with the *Naked* practices share her thoughts. Here is an introduction to the book from Alexis Shepard, ActionCoach Executive Recruiter:

As salespeople, we risk hundreds, thousands, sometimes millions of dollars every time we open our mouths.

Packed with product knowledge, passion, and enthusiasm, we pick up the phone, take the stage, sit down to lunch meetings, and stand face to face with potential buyers everyday. We do our very best to represent our products and services, our companies, and ourselves in a respectable manner.

We've been taught to ask great questions and promote our products with a motivated and positive image. While all this is important and effective, the reality is: *If your confidence, credibility, and technique are built solely on your product knowledge and one-on-one selling skills, you are missing a critical element of influence.*

We know that, while people love to buy, they don't like being sold to. We also know that people will not remember what you did or said, but how you made them *feel*. That being said, one-on-one selling skills alone will never convert as many prospects as possible.

When you reach within yourself and present confidently, you inspire your customers to buy.

So there it is. Every time you open your mouth, you're selling something. If it's your own business vision or your company's products and services, not much happens until somebody buys. You may have been missing out on some serious cash by avoiding (or butchering) a compelling sales presentation opportunity. Since decision-makers sometimes run in herds, you may have to stampede them to the sale.

Thousands of books have been written on influence and persuasion—even on seduction—as it applies to sales. This one takes the best of all those approaches. Then it adds a bit of creativity, yielding several easy-to-remember tools that you can use every day to bring you closer to your own dream of professional success.

Chapter 1

OVERCOMING THE OVEREXPOSURE

SALES SITUATION When I'm asked to make a sales pitch to a large group, I feel so exposed.

> The room is filled with people chatting with each other, e-mailing from their BlackBerries, and sipping coffee. You survey the group for a friendly face or an expectant look, but all you see is irritation and boredom. As you approach the head of the conference table, your stomach twists and cramps, you feel sweat roll down your sides. Your shaking hand reaches for a glass of water to help your dry mouth. You . . .

STOP!

That's not you—not anymore, that is. Not after you begin practicing the techniques you will learn in this book. After developing the skills of a *Naked Salesperson,* you will have experiences that play out like this:

> People are coming into the room. You're smiling, shaking hands with each one, calling some by name. They get their

coffee, and as they sit down they ensure that they've turned off their mobile phones. You walk through the group, nodding a greeting to each person as you head to the front of the room. Completely enthused about your product and your desire to help the audience understand its importance, you wait impatiently for the introduction.

Throughout your pitch your mind is calculating the next story or fact you want to use; your strategy is playing out in the attentive faces fixed on you. You handle each question deftly because you have already anticipated it and have a great response that further supports your goals. And at the end, they applaud. Not only do they applaud, the head buyer approaches you and says, "Sounds great! Where do I sign?"

Speak Well to Sell Well

One of the reasons that we fear making a pitch in front of a large group is that we have no idea how to prepare material, present strategically, or answer questions quickly and correctly. In truth, we create most of our own bad impressions, and frankly, the negative reception that we receive is just because we don't know any better.

> **SalesPEAK Secret:** We create most of our own bad impressions.

The best communicators win. The less interference there is between you and your audience, the more likely you are to get to them to purchase your product or service. We should be working on electrifying our conversations and presentations, not insulating ourselves in protective layers of technology and distance. When we layer on so many trappings, we keep our great ideas from moving out into the world and risk alienating others in the process.

NAKED TIP: People who speak well:

- Gain positive and significant attention
- Create and keep quality professional relationships
- Make the big sales

When you choose to *sell naked*, you remove all of the cumbersome distractions and free yourself to achieve two of the most driving ambitions of any successful salesperson:

1. To be completely understood
2. To get the buy you want

Consider some of the greatest speakers of all time, like John F. Kennedy, Winston Churchill, and Martin Luther King Jr. Even though you probably never saw any of these orators speak in person, you can study their tapes, their transcripts, and consider their verbal and nonverbal commonalities to determine what connects each of them as highly respected speakers. Learn from the way these great speakers conducted themselves, and adapt that confident style to the way you pitch your product.

Model Speakers

According to the consumer review website Rate It All (*www.rateitall.com*), following are the top ten greatest orators:

- John F. Kennedy
- Winston Churchill
- Martin Luther King Jr.
- Franklin D. Roosevelt
- Mahmoud Ahmadinejad
- Bill Clinton
- Tony Blair
- Eleanor Roosevelt
- Adolf Hitler
- Ronald Reagan

Many of us assume that what each of these speakers has in common is a mystical charisma that cannot be emulated. However, what we can *observe* from watching their tapes and reading their transcripts is that in order to be an effective speaker, you need to be organized, passionate, and able to make people believe in what you want them to believe. Like them, you can learn to use carefully chosen words, a strong passionate voice, and techniques to engage audiences' attention for extended periods of time.

Speak Naked

Remember that dream you have occasionally? The one where you're out in public somewhere—be it at work, the gym, or walking down the street—and you're naked? While you might be one of the few that finds it exciting and liberating, it is an excruciatingly uncomfortable situation for most of us; that same level of discomfort can be achieved by standing up in front of a group to give a pitch, or even sitting one-on-one with an intimidating buyer asking him for a sale.

NAKED SALESPERSON STUDY: Glenda

A very competent medical technology salesperson, Glenda is one such example of a person who thought she was protecting herself by using all types of presentation aids to support her sale. She was invited to meet with a large group of buyers at a medical technology conference. It started off fine, and she walked through her many slides explaining the advantages of her company's latest tool.

Suddenly, Glenda's PowerPoint application quit out of nowhere. She fumbled through her notes as the audience patiently waited. And waited. Becoming distraught, Glenda tried valiantly to pick up where the PowerPoint presentation left off.

Unfortunately, Glenda's pitch stopped in its tracks because she became paralyzed by fear. She knew her topic thoroughly, was familiar with the audience, yet she depended on her hardware and was completely lost when it unexpectedly quit on her.

Glenda is just one example of how the layers of technology that we have come to rely on to protect us from embarrassment during our sales calls actually prevent the one element that would make us successful: an intimate mental connection to the buyer.

What do you do when you are dropped into a situation like that? Do you run for cover and try to hide behind all sorts of things? Is your pitch reliant on technological aids and other smoke-and-mirrors-type props? For work presentations we use a PowerPoint full of slides so we don't have to speak to anyone. We wear our custom-made suits and hope to secure credibility by the way we look. Whenever we speak in public, we require portable electronics, keyboards, wireless devices, lighted pointers, and Internet video. Never in history have there been so many devices and services to support a sales presentation. Yet we are much like the child whose mother loads him up in seven layers of clothes and a snowsuit to protect him from frostbite. The child is warm and protected, but he's too bundled up to effectively have any fun in the snow.

This book's purpose is to start a revolution to start developing true, human relations in making sales pitches. As speaking coaches, we intend to elevate your effectiveness in sales situations so you *can* get what you want! Becoming a *Naked Salesperson* isn't about walking down the street with no clothes; it's about becoming a confident salesperson who has a stripped-down approach to making the sale.

It's about . . .

- Breaking down all the barricades we have put up to protect ourselves during pitches
- Stripping away the layers that separate us from our buyers when we go on sales calls
- Achieving mental intimacy with your buyer—you're in their head; they're in yours

Don't worry. This is *not* an epiphany book—you won't be expected to chant a mantra then suddenly demonstrate the power to captivate your audience and rack up those purchase orders. We're going to take small, reasonable steps. You have spent most of your professional life convincing yourself that you need all sorts of presentation materials in order to be an effective salesperson. However, approaching presentations with *The Naked Salesperson* strategy, you will gradually realize that you alone are in control of the outcomes.

SalesPEAK Secret: Becoming a *Naked Salesperson* isn't about walking down the street with no clothes; it's about becoming a confident salesperson who has a stripped-down approach to making the sale.

Each small change you make will bring you closer to becoming the salesperson you want to be.

The Birth of a New Perspective

When we're born, we are all naked and we are all equal. At birth we are without clothing, speech, or bladder control—more importantly though, we are without worry. We cry when we are hungry and expect someone to bring us food. We coo when we are happy and expect people to continue rocking us. We scream when we are soiled and expect our parents to change us. In these situations, a baby never worries about whether his tie is straight, his grammar is correct, or his buyer is interested in his product.

This is naked communication—basic, purposeful, and generally very effective.

Little children, up to six or seven years of age, are still pretty unguarded. Just ask any parents about the time their child said something like, "Phew! Don't Grandpa's farts stink!" in public—and in front of Grandpa.

Shortly after that, though, come the teenage years, when scrutiny overshadows spontaneity. It's a time when every sentence spoken to them is pounced upon with, "Hey, why'd you say that?" Or, "Did you hear what she said? Hah, what a loser." At this adolescent stage, peer approval becomes even more critical than effectiveness.

And then it's all downhill from there in terms of communicating effectively. As adults we dread speaking at meetings, presenting to our bosses, answering difficult questions, and talking to people we don't know. But these are not things that we can just shy away from while accepting our failures to connect as inevitable. We make these situations worse when we voice our negative expectations to the audience.

Don't Settle for Second-Best

Settling for unsatisfying exchanges in your professional life is unacceptable and ultimately unhealthy. This particular brand of consensual misery can lead to failures in your career. If you lack the ability to communicate effectively with another person, it's likely that you will feel:

- Aggravated
- Frustrated

- Unhappy
- Helpless
- Obsessively needy

When you choose to settle rather than to strive to do your best, it negatively affects your entire life. Not only will you not make the sale, but your professional unhappiness will transfer to general unhappiness, too. This unhappiness will ultimately eat away at your life.

NAKED SALESPERSON STUDY: Fred

In one sales situation, the star salesperson from a *Fortune* 500 company was called away at the last minute due to a family emergency. Fred, one of the company's mid-level salespeople, was sent as the substitute. The first words out of his mouth when he entered the conference room where he was to give a group sales presentation were: "Well, sorry, but Linda was called to New York, so you have me and I'm really not prepared for this."

Fred just told his group of buyers that a miserable time was coming and that he didn't really respect them enough to earnestly prepare a meaningful pitch. As you might guess, there were audible groans from the group. The reality is that perhaps Fred could have been a more compelling and engaging salesperson than Linda. But he lost any credibility and power by admitting his discomfort from the beginning.

We limit our success potential unnecessarily when we remain clumsy in our speaking situations, especially when help is available.

You think we're exaggerating? How many times have you smoked an extra cigarette because you were nervous about an important presentation? Or taken that extra drink? Or gone home and sat in front of the television to eat chocolate because a sales call didn't go well?

NAKED SALESPERSON STUDY: Jack

Consider Jack, a typically anxious salesperson. Just before any pitch, Jack isn't able to get to sleep and finds himself groggy and irritable just before a morning presentation. In addition, he dashes out without breakfast and instead of drinking his typical two cups of coffee, he downs three or four.

After that much coffee consumed on an empty stomach, and with his anxiety adding to it, Jack makes his sales pitch looking like "the Energizer Bunny on crack," according to his boss.

Jack does not take the time to properly prepare himself before his pitches, and therefore he gets nervous. His nerves disrupt his sleep pattern. His lack of sleep causes him to become hopped-up on caffeine. See how this is a vicious circle? Jack needs to change his professional lifestyle in order to better his whole life.

Maybe it's worse and you let your inability to interact with others—except behind the anonymity of online conversations and a two-hundred-slide PowerPoint pitch—take over your life.

STOP!

You need to accept the fact that you can do something about this inability to communicate properly. You can take on a new, naked perspective that allows you to stop the aggravation and frustration, stop feeling unhappy and helpless, and stop turning to unhealthy alternatives to compensate for a bad pitch.

Situational Speaking

Many people think that some are born with a special gene for exceptional verbal ability—and that they aren't one of those people. While some do have a natural ability, effective communication of any sort is a learned skill. Science tells us that we all have multiple talents in different areas. Some can sing; others are good at sports. But even if you can't naturally sing like a pop star, you can learn to do better than that dog howl that comes out when you attempt to sing along with the radio. You can develop new skills.

Situational speaking skill is what we're talking about here. You can learn methods that will make you feel relaxed and in control in different types of speaking conditions.

Fear in Formal Situations

Formal speaking situations where you're in front of a large group of people, such as during group pitches, company meetings, or social networking events and fundraisers, all have one common element—you feeling exposed in front of a crowd. Though we speak to multiple people every day, something is different when they're all grouped together in a room looking at you.

We'd all really love to have a crowd of admirers: people smiling and applauding, waving to us, making us feel comfortable standing up there. But too often your group of listeners seems like an angry mob, like the villagers with clubs and torches chasing Frankenstein into the woods. Even if it's a meeting with just your sales team—Alan, Rashid, Erica, and Michael—for some reason, when you have to formally present to them, they become like that group of nameless, faceless strangers with clubs and torches.

Break It Down to What You're Used To

We have all been speaking to people one-on-one our entire lives, so we're okay with that kind of communication. Every one of these exchanges, though, is a presentation or pitch of some sort. You personally give fifty or more mini-presentations a day. They may go something like this:

"Let's get on the slopes, the snow is great!"	**Motivational**
"Anna, can you drop me off at the train station? I'll get to the gym faster that way."	**Persuasive**
"Hey, we just reached our quota—and two months early!"	**Good news**
"Hmmmm. Let's see. You might try using multiple open windows on the screen so the customer information will be right there for you."	**Training**
"No, this isn't going to work for me. I need another lease car by this afternoon. My boss wants me to drive to Minneapolis and get there by 6:00. What are our alternatives?"	**Negotiation**
"My apologies. Our computers were down in the warehouse so we're experiencing a one-day delay."	**Bad news**

You're okay with the day-to-day exchanges because you know what to say and how those will likely go over. It is *fear* of the unknown that creates your negative attitude about conducting a successful sales pitch. You are *unsure* how the buyer will respond, so you freak out and hide behind your slides, your notes, and the lectern.

SalesPEAK Secret: It is *fear* of the unknown that creates your negative attitude about conducting a successful sales pitch.

NAKED **SALESPERSON STUDY:** Suzanne

One particular case where being physically hidden created a problem was that of Suzanne, who was selling a product to a group of representatives from various companies. She must have been 4'9" in high heels, and most podiums are designed for speakers who are the size of Michael Jordan. Because she was so diminutive in stature, she would have been far better off conducting her pitch in front or to the side of the lectern.

However, she spoke for twenty minutes behind it, almost completely hidden. The microphone hid her nose, and she appeared to be sinking into quicksand. It was not her height but her own need to keep a barrier between her and the audience in order to prevent feeling exposed that caused her sales presentation to go very badly.

Get Naked

When you start integrating the techniques of naked selling that you will learn throughout this book into all your sales calls, pitching in front of groups will feel just as natural and predictable as your day-to-day correspondence with family and friends. This happens because you will know how to *create* positive outcomes. A good impression is no accident. When selling naked, you don't have to worry and stress over:

- How do I look?
- Will they believe me?
- How can I get agreement?
- Do they like me?
- Can they understand? (This stuff is pretty complicated.)
- Am I interesting and persuasive?

An effective naked salesperson uses the processes outlined in the following chapters to demystify the sales pitch and eliminate all your unnecessary concerns—follow the process, and you will be effective.

Be a Better You

If you're reading this book looking to become better at making sales, chances are you aren't one of those silver-tongued salespeople. You know, the type of professionals who are born with that charismatic, sexy kind of appeal in front of groups. They are natural speakers and win over any audience that hears them. This is a tiny number of people.

However, even if you weren't born with silver-tongue talent, you can at least best those salespeople who simply talk their buyers to death with a continuous blah . . . blah . . . b lah. This type of sales rep just loves to talk and enjoys the attention he receives in front of a group. He's not in the sales game because he wants to sell a product; he's in the sales game because it's all about him. Salespeople like this use the audience of buyers as a way to rattle on and on in a self-involved, random brain dump that bores everyone in the room. Not nervous, but not effective either. In short, they stink.

But you, with positive expectations and the techniques of the naked salesperson, can *wow* any audience of buyers—you just need some help.

Name the Demon

An old adage says that if you can name the demons that create torment in your life, you dilute their power over you. We intend to not just dilute but completely banish those demons that hinder your ability to pull together a successful pitch. Here are some typical excuses that you may be using on yourself as a result of those haunting demons:

"I just found out I have to give a presentation and I don't have a clue where to start."

"This is a tough group. They look like they don't want to be here."

"They're not listening."

"No one seems to get what I'm saying."

"What if they attack me with their questions?"

"Now that I'm finished, I need to get a commitment."

NAKED SALESPERSON STUDY: John

Let's take a look at John. When he makes a pitch in front of a group of prospective buyers, he feels the need to hurry up and finish so he can eliminate the pain that he is feeling as a result of his fear. Therefore, he speaks rapidly, so quickly, in fact, that the customers get lost in the first few sentences. He nervously waves his arms around while pacing about the room. The buyers tune him out from irritation, while he exhibits his anxiety in front of them.

This is a demonstration of his primal desire to flee the situation and hide.

When we meet demons—whether they are of the real lions and tigers and bears variety or simply phantoms in our head, our body becomes alert to the situation, and our survival default system takes over.

This is a natural, instinctive, human response to danger, and it shows up in the form of:

- Releasing of cortisol in the brain
- Pumping of adrenaline to the system
- Rerouting of blood to the muscles

These physiological changes result in:

- Suppression of analytical thinking
- Hands shaking or sweating
- Rapid and shallow breathing
- Nausea or butterflies
- Rapid speech
- An intense need to run or fight

The body's response to fear of embarrassment or psychological pain is exactly the same as its response to a potential physical threat from an enemy. The expectation of failure frightens us, and that paralyzing fear spoils the chances of successfully closing a deal.

To see how this plays out in a room full of decision makers, consider the following behaviors that police officers look for to determine if someone is lying.

- Limited, stiff physical expression, with few arm and hand movements
- Hand, arm, and leg movements toward the person's own body, thus taking up less space
- Avoidance of eye contact
- Touching the face, throat, and mouth
- Touching or scratching the nose or behind their ear

Sound familiar? This is exactly the way you behave when you are uncomfortable during your sales pitch. If the buyer reads your nervous body language, then she will not believe what you say. You have in effect sabotaged your own presentation. And frankly, she doesn't care if you're nervous; she has come to this meeting looking to purchase a new product or service, not deal with your issues. Though a buyer may feel sympathy for you if you have a great deal of difficulty during your pitch, it will be a pained sympathy with irritation over her own wasted time, and you will not get the buy.

Naked Scenarios

Throughout the book we will illustrate our naked lessons by walking you through the pitches of Kyle—a bike engineer who needs to fine-tune his product pitch—and Lindsay—a service contractor who has to give her first group pitch. Just like you, these two need help. And just like you, they will receive the help they need by following the N-A-K-E-D approach.

Kyle's Story

"A young engineer with a plan" is what the local paper called Kyle with his two new bicycle designs geared toward the Boomer market. His concept is to develop two bicycles: one targets the middle-aged, exercise-conscious people who have either given up running due to joint issues or who want to become fit and enjoy the outdoors; the other is a stunt, BMX-style bike that these same people could buy for their grandchildren. The product names are Crosswyse Cross-Trainer and Crosswyse CrossTrick. With the goal of selling to outdoor recreation chains, Kyle will have to make presentations to financial backers, at trade shows and, hopefully, to international dealers.

"So, what's the problem?" asked Kyle's business manager and head of marketing, Brian.

"I'm a techie, I can't give a pitch. You're the marketing guy—can't you do it?"

"Okay, let's go through this again. About half the people we will be meeting with really know the nuts and bolts of bike construction. I can set up the appointments, get the groups together, but, frankly, those guys won't want to hear my stuff and the ones who sign the checks won't budge until the hands-on people give their okay. Got it now?" Brian explained.

"Yeah, I know, but that's not really my thing." Kyle glanced down uncomfortably.

"Well, get over it. There's a lot on the line here. Look, I can set you up with a presentation coach. I'll make an appointment for four o'clock. Be here."

* * *

The coach showed up, right on time. "Kyle, are you ready to go to work and build this presentation?"

"What do I have to do? Brian tells me that you can turn me into some kind of smooth salesman."

"I can help you develop your message and deliver it so that the important decision-makers will listen. The rest will be up to you and the merits of your products. Can we get started?" The coach began.

For the next forty minutes Kyle wrote down ideas, gathered drawings and photos of his prototypes, and pulled together everything he wanted to get across to prospective dealers. Then, the coach challenged him, "Now, Kyle, using what you have here—your design philosophy, the photos and drawings and the prototypes—give me a ten-minute rundown on why a dealer might want to carry your line. While you're talking, I'll get it all on video."

Kyle's eyes widened. "You want me to do what? And you're going to *recall* it all?" Kyle's stomach tightened and he froze.

"We have to start somewhere, and this is as good a time as any." The coach explained.

Finally able to speak, Kyle offered in a strained voice, "Can't we just put together a slide presentation and run it?"

The coach gave a little laugh and shook her head, "No way."

Lindsay's Story

"Here it is, Lindsay. I heard from one of my networking contacts that the Hansen & Gruen Insurance Company has been having a lot of trouble with their contract helpdesk operation and they're shopping around for a new contractor. We've got an in, so . . . it's going to be your first big client presentation." Michelle, her manager, said with an eager smile, expecting Lindsay to be thrilled.

"My *what*? I've only ever sold one-on-one; I've never done a group pitch. Why me?"

"Because you're our brightest star." Michelle gestured in a large flourish pointing both hands toward Lindsay as if she were introducing the next act on stage.

"And you think I'm ready to present to such a huge account?" Lindsay asked.

"You will be soon." She grinned.

* * *

Muttering to herself as she went over her service benefits sheet, Lindsay fretted, *what do they expect of me? I've never done anything like this. I can't stand up in front of a roomful of people at such a huge firm. I nearly puked going to the front of the room to get my sales award.*

She got up and walked to the window, giving herself a pep talk. "Lindsay, you are a professional. You've been the number one sales rep in the region for the last two quarters. It's not really any different than talking one-on-one with a rep from a smaller firm with smaller stakes . . . is it?"

She trudged back to her desk and slumped into her chair. Leaning forward onto the desk, she cradled her head in her hands as she broke out in a cold sweat. "Yes, it is *very* different," she said aloud in her misery. "I need some help."

Pulling her cell phone out of her purse, she quickly scanned the contact list and pressed SEND. "Alexis, hi, it's Lindsay."

"Hey! What's up?" Alexis, Lindsay's former college roommate answered cheerily.

"You still work for that training company, don't you? The one that helps salespeople look better?"

"I wouldn't exactly put it that way, but yes, I'm doing sales-coaching," Alexis explained.

"What would it take for you to help me get ready for a presentation that could be a $100,000-a-year gig for my company—if I can pull it off?" Lindsay tried not to sound like she was pleading.

"I'd have to do it after-hours, but I'd do that for you."

"Thanks, you'll save my butt, and I'll owe you one." Lindsay promised.

"Oh yeah you will." Alexis snickered. "The first thing you need to do is get your head on straight about the situation. You can do this; it's not like you don't tell people about your company's benefits every day. We're just going to help you do it standing up."

"That is if I don't faint!" Lindsay moaned.

"Lindsay, I'll get you counting those bonus dollars soon. You're going to be great!"

Lindsay started thinking through the challenge. *This is such a competitive situation because the client has proprietary software that could be time consuming for our team to learn. How can I get past Michael who really favors the competition? If I'm going to get promoted, I really need to close this business.*

Then she remembered Alexis's suggestion. *I've got a lot of data about their situation and look at this website. It's a formal company, pretty traditional, German owned, and based in Hartford. The photos of the principals in the company are all shown in dark suits; their history is that they bring in the best.* Lindsay continued to study their website. *Hmmm. On the media pages they are announcing new growth in their community involvement and are very proud of this initiative. The corporate report refers to a new blog that the company is setting up to field customer inquiries and provide more information on services.*

She sat back in her chair to reflect for a moment. *This is a perfect match. We have the right service tools and this should go great. Maybe I really can pull this off.* Lindsay smiled to herself, but five minutes later the cold sweat came back . . .

The Naked Solution to Fear

The process that the naked salesperson uses will peel away the nervous, self-sabotaging layers that separate your pitch from your buyers. It establishes a natural mental intimacy between you and the buyer, while ensuring that you are understood and taken seriously.

The following chapters will look at each of the threats to a positive sales delivery. And they will show you how to make presenting to a group feel easy and natural. Here is a guide to lead you through presentations that both you and your customers will find engaging.

You will:

Navigate the situation by building a plan.
Approach the sale and the audience with enthusiasm.
Keep your buyer with you throughout your pitch.
Engage questioners with message matching and management.
Drive the *do* and get the buy.

By understanding how to make each and every career-related presentation go well, you can relax and gain confidence in your strategic advantage. Before you know it, you too will be able to sell naked without feeling exposed.

Chapter 2

START FROM THE BEGINNING

SALES SITUATION: I just found out I have to give a major sales presentation, and I don't have a clue where to start.

> Imagine that you are sailing a forty-foot yacht through the Caribbean. Your plan is to visit several islands, soak up the sun, and party with the locals. Ahh, now that's a vacation. That is, unless you haven't charted your route, planned what to wear to the parties, or phoned ahead for reservations at the Conch Bistro.

Even fun requires some thinking ahead. And once you are clear on how to navigate your presentations, you'll find they're lots of fun. This chapter will look at the Navigation part of the N-A-K-E-D process.

Your first order of business in navigating your presentation is to plan to succeed. You'll want to call on the creative part of your brain to start this navigation process. Problem solving can feel negative and draining; vacation planning inspires and energizes us. Which is a better feeling? Which do you think you will accomplish faster? You need to be in the right frame of mind in order to plan your pitch. Don't dread it. It's much easier if you approach your selling situation in that positive zone. Focus on trying to create the inspiration you feel when planning a vacation—not the dread that overcomes you when you are problem solving.

> **SalesPEAK** Secret: You need to be in the right frame of mind in order to plan your pitch.

Now that you're in the right frame of mind, let's get you ready to put together a compelling presentation.

N—Navigate the sale by creating a plan.

Checking Out the Scene

As you think about your presentation, you must determine:

- What does your product/service have to offer to your buyers?
- Who is the key person you need to appeal to in your presentation?
- Why/how are your listeners going to be turned on by your pitch?

This last element is particularly significant because if *you* can't come up with an edge to your sales presentation, your customer certainly won't care to listen or buy.

Whatever the occasion or formal purpose of your presentation is, the naked salesperson creates natural, positive connections with audiences. In this way *your* ideas become *theirs*, your products become theirs, and the money they have budgeted becomes yours! When this process occurs, you don't have to work so hard to get the results you want.

> **SalesPEAK Secret:** Whatever the occasion or formal purpose of your presentation is, the naked salesperson creates natural, positive connections with audiences.

What Do You Have to Offer?

Before anything else, you need to think about what you're actually selling. Assess what part of your product/service is really what your customer needs to hear about in order to make a decision in your favor. You've been asked to present for a reason. This is a *compliment*.

In a selling situation, it is also a gift. Unless the customer thought you had a possible solution or improvement to offer, you wouldn't have been given the slot of time to do your thing.

Someone thinks you have valuable ideas that others need to hear. Talk with the person who has asked you to pitch. Find out:

- What *exactly* is needed?
- Who are key decision makers?
- What is the extent of this sales opportunity?

In other words, you need to know what needs to happen for you to be successful. This is the basis for building your picture of a "happy ending." Most formal presentations—be it a sales pitch or just a company meeting—are not for "information" only. Information is just data that could be sent to the necessary parties via e-mail. If you've been invited to speak, you're expected to achieve a result. You are not just delivering information; you are conveying knowledge. The ability to convey knowledge—and what the listener is supposed to do with that knowledge—is a separate strategy. Think of it as your pickup plan; to be successful you must "pick up" people that will support your product/service.

Scoping Out the Group

Next, review the profiles of the people who you'll be selling to. Remember that you will be *with* them, not isolated in front of them. The more *with* them you are during your presentation, the more likely they will be *with* you at the end. In short, you are going to need a way to engage them. Since different groups have different interests, you must understand who your buyers truly are and where they're coming from.

> **SalesPEAK** Secret: You must understand who your buyers truly are and where they're coming from.

Consider the profile of the person to whom you're making the pitch. Is he young or old? Is she knowledgeable of the field or not? Have they bought from you before? These are all important questions that should be answered while you're navigating your pitch plan. You should find out the following about your buyers *before* making your pitch in order to construct a profile of whom you're selling to:

- Age range
- Frame of mind (are they optimistic or pessimistic?)
- Educational background
- Knowledge of your company
- Professional background
- Current job status (are they junior or senior buyers?)

If you're presenting to a large group of people, you need to identify who are the really attractive ones. These are the people to whom you should be appealing. Obviously, we don't mean "attractive" in the physical sense. We mean attractive in the sense that these are the decision makers and the ones with the most influence over the group. This is why you need to do your homework and scope out the group members. The person with the most seniority is not always the most attractive. You want the people with the most sway over the group to be your advocates. These are the people that you need to focus your pitch on.

SalesPEAK Secret: You want the people with the most sway over the group to be your advocates.

Typical Turn-Ons

Turn-ons are often just a matter of strategic phrasing, or a presentation style used for a specific group of buyers. Depending on your industry, you can tailor your pitches to include specific turn-ons that will make your presentation more appealing. Let's look at some buzzwords and presentation aids that are turn-ons for different types of customers.

GENERAL BUSINESS AUDIENCE TURN-ONS

- "Cost-saving"
- "Return on investment"
- "Reduced expenses"
- "Gaining market share"
- "Driving revenue"
- Using a succinct PowerPoint presentation

TECHNICAL AUDIENCE TURN-ONS

- "Efficiency"
- "More capacity"
- "Fewer bugs"
- Using charts, tables, formulas, test results, and graphs
- Using handouts (preferably together in a binder with an index and a table of contents)

PROJECT MANAGERS TURN-ONS

- "On time"
- "In budget"
- "Dedicated resources"
- The preparation and availability of a backup plan

Once you are in the heads of your anticipated audience, the next step takes place in your own head. It's time to get creative and brainstorm.

Fire Up Your Brain Bursts

When you allow your creativity to emerge, the thoughts generated will include things that you already know or think about your product or service as well as new ways to think about and package it. The information that you have gained by talking to the people who were involved in coming up with the product/service, or by conducting your own research, will come into play to get your ideas flowing. During your brainstorming sessions, you want to allow your ideas to just flow without constraint.

> **SalesPEAK** Secret: During your brainstorming sessions, you want to allow your ideas to just flow without constraint.

We call this welling up of thoughts a *brain burst* because it should shoot out and onto your pitch notes like fireworks. A healthy brainstorming session will result in a number of brain bursts and should get you excited about your presentation. These sessions should help you to figure out why the customer desperately needs your company's product/service.

If you are stumped trying to put thoughts on paper, shift to another medium. Examples include finding a room in your office with a whiteboard and scribbling down your thoughts across the much bigger medium, or stepping outside for fresh air with a voice-recorder and recording your thoughts as you take a stroll. Remember, this is supposed to be a creative time. If you fire off brain bursts with abandon and aren't worried whether those thoughts or ideas are any good, you'll find that your planning time will take only about five to ten minutes because while all your thoughts might not be usable, you'll have generated a surplus of them and be able to choose the really good ones.

Remember that everything in your brain has the same value to you, so ideas explode at random in a variety of sizes, shapes, and colors. As the ideas explode onto your planning page, don't worry about the order until *after* the fireworks—just let them explode. Our brains are random storage facilities. When we try to pull things out in a linear, stepwise manner, our retrieval processes go into overload. It's best to create two separate steps in this brainstorming process: idea creation and then idea ordering.

SalesPEAK Secret: It's best to create two separate steps in this brainstorming process: idea creation and then idea ordering.

After you have filled a page or whiteboard with your brain burst notes, you will start the N-A-K-E-D organization process.

NAKED TIP: Inspiring and influencing decisions involves delivering what your clients (even if it's only one) need through a passionate connection. You want to evoke some sort of action: Unless they *feel* something, they won't *do* anything.

Organizing Strategically

Every presentation situation requires several key strategic parts. For this reason, you should arrange your brain bursts in the order you will present. You are truly a naked salesperson when you can:

- Engage the buyer's attention
- Touch on three key features of your product/service
- Answer follow-up questions skillfully
- Motivate your buyers to a commitment

You see? Putting together a sales presentation is just a matching game—match the client's needs with the key features of your products or services. Once you've used your brain burst time to determine what in fact those key features are, you just need to spend some time fashioning them into a tight pitch by organizing them in such a way that the buyer will find the connection natural and easy to act on.

If you've ever heard anyone speak off the cuff, you know how important organization is for listeners. Speaking without organization creates more of a brain *barf*. And quite frankly, no one appreciates being "barfed" on. Listeners will quickly look for an escape strategy out of the situation. You've experienced those presentations before: the salesperson spews forth all of his product knowledge, as well as any random thoughts that happen to occur, at the speed of light, never pausing to take a breath. Then the listener is left to sort out if anything useful was said. You don't want confused buyers; you want interested, decisive customers. Therefore, it is extremely important to review the ideas you came up with during your brainstorming session and then take the time to choose and organize the ones that will help sell your product/service the best.

> **SalesPEAK Secret:** It is extremely important to review the ideas you came up with during your brainstorming session and then take the time to choose and organize the ones that will help sell your product/service the best.

Send Your Buyer an Irresistible Invitation

To have a successful party, you have to entice people to come. Right? Selling is no different. Your opening consists of two parts: engaging everyone's concentration and setting up an expectation for the sale. You only have about ten seconds to accomplish this task, and it's a critically important one.

Naked selling connects you with your buyer. Initiating this connection requires you to invite customers to join you as participants in a conversation. Fearful sales reps try to stay separate from their group of prospective buyers; they avoid that intimacy. Thus, they create an endless number of slides, mountains of useless handouts, and a stack of fifty note cards from which they read directly. By doing this, they alienate themselves from the people who make the decisions—the very ones that salespeople need to reach!

An invitation welcomes your buyers to your presentation and helps to immediately make a naked connection between you and them. The best invitations include:

A story related to a customer need or to the effectiveness of your product: for example, "Sir James Dyson tried to make a bagless vacuum that sucks (in a good way). It took him 5,126 tries, and he nearly went bankrupt while pursuing his dream. Today, he is one of the richest men in Britain."

An unexpected or shocking statement: "We're expecting record numbers of customers to call in the next quarter, which can only mean you're going to need an extra forty machines immediately to handle the volume."

A question that engages your audience: "What is it that bugs you the most about your software application?"

A surprising statistic: "Seventy-four percent of new managers fail within eighteen months."

A relevant prop: as the rep tips an hourglass, he says, "See the sand running through this hour glass? It's exactly like what's happening to your profits. Time may be draining away . . ."

A costume: wearing a hat, a colorful vest, a pair of gloves, or anything unconventional will draw unexpected attention and allow you to follow with, "The next time I wear this cap, I expect to be lounging around a pool with an ice cold beer in one hand and a bottle of Hawaiian Tropic in the other. Will you be with me on the celebration trip?"

Music: playing music as your client group comes into the speaking room can set the tone and redirect attention (just don't sing!). For example, playing "(I Can't Get No) Satisfaction" by the Rolling Stones may be a fun way to kick off a customer service initiative. Or maybe Daniel Powter's "Had a Bad Day" to suggest that their competition is going to suffer.

Also, using humor is an effective beginning, though not in the form of jokes. You can use something relevant from the news that day, commentary on the group that the buyers will find funny, or possibly a tie-in to a recent activity they will relate to. Self-deprecating humor also works well. After all, if you can handle being made fun of, you are immediately more approachable and likable.

Separate from the Pack—in a Good Way

To gain attention in nature, animals have a number of different adaptations that make them stand out. Birds have rich, multihued plumage; wolves have a dance; elephants trumpet; and macaques have bright red butts. Now think, what have *you* got that will get you and your product/service noticed by the buyer? (No, painting your bottom red and mooning the audience is not an option . . . although sometimes tempting.)

Sometimes salespeople will have a shtick that gets them attention from the buyers, but not in a positive light (think painting your behind red). You want to be sure that the way you choose to set yourself apart from the competition doesn't set you apart in a *bad* way.

SalesPEAK Secret: You want to be sure that the way you choose to set yourself apart from the competition doesn't set you apart in a *bad* way.

Here are some invitations that will ultimately leave you off the list at the next party.

INVITATIONS TO AVOID

- Jokes—most people are poor joke tellers, and the joke also might offend someone; or worse, it could bomb with everybody because it's not funny and now you've got to use the remaining forty minutes to try and reel them back in. You're not David Letterman, so don't pretend.
- Cliché openers—"How are you?" and "Good Morning" are expected and lame; get on with it!
- Chatting your way to the front of the room—it seems phony; step up, pause, then jump in.
- Dictionary definitions—boring and amateurish
- Self-introductions—"Hello, my name is Yoda and I have two PhDs and am well versed in . . ." The focus needs to be on your product/service, not you.
- Cartoons on a slide—overdone, out of context, and not an effective opener.

Plan your opening and practice it. A lot. This is the part of your message that you need to memorize because it is so important to set the stage for the sale. The opening is your one shot. Think of your opening as a pickup line. You want to create an instant connection between you and the buyer you are attempting to court. If you aren't confident in what you're going to say and how you're going to say it, you are going to lose their attention. An opening needs to be strong, because as with a pickup line, if it isn't, you're going home alone.

When buyers come to listen to your pitch, they most likely are not just thinking about you or your product. They have been working on a number of other things that day and have a million other deadlines and thoughts and issues floating around in their heads. You have to win buyers over from the get-go so that you become their focus.

> **SalesPEAK** Secret: You have to win buyers over from the get-go so that you become their focus.

For this reason, you've got just those first few seconds to capture them and set the stage for a successful sale. You have to create anticipation for something pleasant and satisfying to come. That way, you are more likely to get a "yes" when it comes to the question of whether or not they're interested in your product/service later in your proposal.

Stating Your Purpose

After the opening invitation comes your *purpose statement* that briefly describes your true objective in the presentation. As you plan your engagement strategy, remember that people like to know the occasion for a party and what is going to happen. In the same way, they want to know what to expect from your talk. Although everyone may have received an agenda before your presentation, buyers forget and, for the most part, don't even care . . . until you engage them!

There are three rules for creating your purpose statement in a sales presentation:

Rule #1: Keep the sentence simple.

Rule #2: Use the second person "you."

Rule #3: Answer the question the buyer's asking herself: "Why should I care?"

Constructing a successful purpose statement that adheres to these three rules is imperative if you want your pitch to be successful. It's important that your statement addresses all three in order to really get the buyer invested in the presentation that's about to start. Here are a couple examples of strong purpose statements:

"Today you'll find out how a minimal investment of 400k will reap benefits of over 800k in the first year."

"The purpose of today's presentation is to disclose the secret recipe for a successful merger."

They are simple. They engage the listener. They make the listener invested in the presentation. Now your decision-makers will *want* to hear what you have to say because your pitch is about them, not you.

> **SalesPEAK Secret:** Constructing a success-
> ful purpose statement that adheres to these
> three rules is imperative if you want your
> pitch to be successful. It's important that
> your statement addresses all three in order
> to really get the buyer invested in the presen-
> tation that's about to start.

When you open with, "Today I'm going to tell you about . . ." your buyers are saying to themselves, "So? Nobody cares about you." Your purpose statement needs to be constructed in terms to which the decision makers will relate.

Bringing the Bare Necessities

Planning to limit what you say is not just a matter of time; it's a matter of effectiveness.

Set up your presentation around three main points, because that's all the audience is taking with them. People remember in threes. By organizing this way, you are removing the pressure of overplanning. Mention these limits in your opening so that you prepare the buyers' brains to take in your points. When your opener says you are going to provide three ways to ensure an on-time project completion, you can focus on the most important three reasons, and by the conclusion, you should get a commitment.

Another important reason for setting up three major bullets for your group is to prevent interruptions. Since they have been alerted to what's about to come, they are less likely to stop you during your presentation with questions, objections, or their own stories that disrupt your flow and tend to distract everyone else.

Also, memorizing a long speech is self-defeating. Memorization is like a chain—if one link breaks, the rest is lost. If you forget one little part, the rest of the ideas that are connected to that will disappear as well. Besides, a memorized spiel is a droning bore. No one wants to hear a canned pitch. Better to know *three* persuasive ideas so thoroughly that you can present them, well, naked.

SalesPEAK Secret: Memorization is like a chain—if one link breaks, the rest is lost.

Organization Is Key

In place of memorizing, you can organize your material using solution guides to help you stay on track. If you are well organized, have a clear train of thought, and plan on covering a manageable amount of information, your pitch will go very smoothly. Rather than worry over whether or not you will recall what you have memorized, you will be focused on the goal set out in your purpose statement.

In order to help with focusing on your goal, you can prepare a number of different presentation aids. These aids will help to cue you in covering only the specific material that needs to be pitched.

Your cue guides can include:

- Note cards with *only* ten keywords
- Flip chart pages
- Acronyms (like the N-A-K-E-D one used in this book)

- Sheets of paper with only eight lines of text in twenty-point font
- Product samples or demonstration objects
- A limited number of slides with only a few words on each (as a last resort)

Each of these presentation aids will help in a different way. Depending on the product or service you're selling, some may not work for your particular presentation. Let's take a closer look at these presentation cues, and you can decide if they will help with your sales pitch.

Note Cards

When using note cards, you should be careful *not* to write out your entire sales presentation in paragraphs, or even sentences. The rule is: the more you write down, the easier it is for your mind to want to depend on reading what you've written. *No one wants to hear you read a presentation.* Buyers hate being read to and anything that canned just pushes the sale farther and farther out of reach.

SalesPEAK Secret: *No one wants to hear you read a presentation.* Buyers hate being read to and anything that canned just pushes the sale farther and farther out of reach.

Resist the urge to write everything out. Instead, stick to only ten words per card as reminders of what you want to convey. Keep in mind that *you* know your content; otherwise, you would not have been asked to make the pitch.

When preparing your note cards, only write on one side of the card. You should also only be writing down keywords that will cue you to relate a larger point of your pitch. Practice giving your pitch and covering all the necessary information using these keywords as prompts. Regardless of how long your pitch is, you should only use *one* card with about ten words on it.

Flip Charts

If presenting to a small group of decision makers (typically fewer than twenty), you can prepare flip chart pages in advance as a skeleton for use during your presentation.

Write your acronym or keywords on the sheets, leaving space to fill in during the presentation itself to make your delivery more interactive and interesting. On your planning checklist, remember to bring your own markers, preferably in dark colors.

SalesPEAK Secret: Using one index card with ten words on it is your guide to staying on track.

Also, if your handwriting is poor, you need to work on your presentation. Practice your penmanship so you do not embarrass yourself or your company during your presentation. You don't want your buyers to think that the flip chart pages were created by your seven-year-old.

NAKED TIP: Any word can be made into an acronym for your presentation. Here is an example:

Navigate the situation by building a plan.

Approach the sale and the audience with enthusiasm.

Keep your buyer with you throughout your pitch.

Engage questioners with message matching and management.

Drive the *do* and get the buy.

Keep acronyms simple and related to your topic. They should make your main points easier to remember, not make the audience work to understand the acronym.

Another idea—if your penmanship is *that* bad—is to print out your flip chart pages on your computer, have them blown up to poster size, and then laminated. This way, you can use a large, reusable, and attractive poster during your presentation. Buyers love this because it's not the same old slide show (like your competitors use), and you can make your delivery interactive with an erasable marker. If you are making this pitch at multiple locations, simply wipe off the notes you write down during any particular presentation, roll the flip chart pages up, and take them to your next presentation.

Paper

A very underrated organizational guide is a standard-size sheet of paper, if it is used correctly. List your main point reminders—with no more than eight lines per sheet in twenty-point font and three line spaces between each keyword. You can generally organize an hour-long speech on two or fewer sheets. Number each line *and* highlight each separate note line with a different color highlighter. We may lose our place in the words, but we generally hold colors well in our memory.

Prepare your two sheets and put them into a folder with the following on the front: your name, the topic, the client, and the time and place of presentation. Pocket folders are the best for these. Remember, notes and not full sentences. And no reading!

Samples and Props

If you're selling a product, it's best to bring along a sample, if available. This will help you to remember to talk about the special features, and it allows the buyers to inspect what they're purchasing.

You could also bring along props that will act as reminders of how you're going to connect your ideas. For example, you can bring in a light bulb and tie it in to rethinking a solution to an IT, staffing, or reorganization problem. A back scratcher could be used to introduce the idea of better teamwork by "scratching each other's backs" to keep the lines of communication open in your client's organization.

Slides

Finally, if you can't avoid it, you can build some slides—but they should *only* contain your basic backbone notes. A fifty-two-slide presentation merely bores people, and slick graphics sometimes just make customers remember the graphic effects—not the product benefits.

Here are some guidelines for effective slide use:

- Make sure they are clean and free of errors, clutter, and excessive words.
- Change slides once every five minutes; you should have no more than ten slides total, and they should be arranged in proper order.
- Each slide should follow the four-by-four rule: no more than four bullets down with a maximum of four words per line.
- Graphics are okay, but be sure they do not distract from the main point.
- Keep your colors and font changes to a minimum to avoid distraction.
- Your room lights should be on during the slide show; the lower the lights, the more potent the invitation to sleep (and not just the buyers—you need to be alert, too!).

Now that you have a handle on the proper use of presentation aids, let's return to the three-point organization system. You understand the importance of honing your pitch to cover the three most important elements of your product/service. However, there needs to be a smooth transition between each point in order to create a cohesive pitch. You must connect one idea to the next in an even, logical fashion. Your audience may be stuck on one point while you merrily trip on to the next. The little salesperson inside your head needs to remember that he is a tour guide, not a lone scout—bring your buyers along with you!

SalesPEAK Secret: You must connect one idea to the next in an even, logical fashion.

Bridge Together Your Presentation

Transitions allow your listeners to easily follow along with you by including closure on one topic and then introducing the next one. Think of your transitions as bridges, linking one stone to another and avoiding the pitfalls.

Constructing an even pitch with smooth transitions takes time and effort. However, if you make sure your transitions make sense and are easy to follow, you should have no problem guiding your buyers along to a sale. Here are a couple examples of strong transitions that bring closure to one point and open the next:

"As we close our discussion of how easy it is to run a franchise operation, let's look at the telecommunications you will need in your new location . . ."

"Timing for a start-up is really important, as we've seen, but next to consider is the investment . . ."

If you know enough transition keywords, a logical pitch is easy to construct. Following the examples above, you can build your own pitch transitions by including these keywords and phrases when necessary:

- First . . .
- Next . . .
- Finally . . .
- In addition to . . .
- And to wrap up . . .

Changing Directions

When you are changing directions, you will need to let the audience know. This is like putting on your blinker when you plan to turn. You want to be especially sure that you do not lose your audience when you change direction. Your presentation could be going great, but all it takes is a wrong turn that confuses the buyers and you've lost them— and the sale.

Following is an example of how a naked salesperson would go about changing direction so he does not lose his audience:

"Since we've looked at all the positive elements in the plan, let's move to the other side and examine the cons."

Similar to building a strong transition, there are certain words and phrases that you can use to help make the direction shift seamless. Try working one of the following into your pitch if you need to change direction:

- In spite of . . .
- Consider this . . .
- But . . .
- Let's flip to a different channel now . . .
- Now, this other viewpoint takes us to . . .
- We looked at A; however, there is another side of the story . . .

A practiced shift will allow the change in direction to seem natural, and not overly prepared.

Practice Makes Perfect

Be sure to plan and practice your transitions and direction changes out loud prior to your delivery. Until you get used to including transition phrases in your speaking, you will want to write them into your notes as reminders—highlight them in color. Remember, you always know what's coming next, but your listeners can get lost if you take a sudden turn.

Transitions help the customers jump with you to your next point. In one-on-one conversations, we don't use transition phrases very much because we can always see if we've lost the connection with the person we are talking to. You can keep a group of buyers with you on a pitch by making sure any changes in direction are clear and easy to follow. Managing transitions well is one element that separates the novice from the skilled naked salesperson.

SalesPEAK Secret: You can keep a group of buyers with you on a pitch by making sure any changes in direction are clear and easy to follow.

Pop the Question

After you've organized your brain bursts into the main points of your speech, review briefly what type of presentation aids you plan on employing, be it an acronym, note cards, or a flip chart. Then prepare for the question-and-answer section. You'll need to maintain control during this portion of your presentation, so preparing for it diligently is crucial.

Because of the importance of managing the question and answer section, rather than truncate it here, we have devoted an entire chapter to it (see Chapter 5). However, we wanted to note that this is the time in the process that you should be preparing for the postpresentation interrogation. Review your purpose statement and pitch, what questions come to your mind? Be sure to have answers to those questions. As mentioned, we'll go into greater detail and supply you with helpful strategies later in the book.

Get 'Em to Say "Yes"

Critical to your success in presentations is leading your audience to say, "Yes, yes, *yes!*" As part of your planning, you'll want to develop your close and practice it over and over again until you nail it. The close must both summarize *and* gain a commitment.

Remember, you are presenting for a reason, so return to your original notes on what your purpose is. An effective close reconnects with the audience on the main points *and* presents the action you need for them to take.

SalesPEAK Secret: An effective close reconnects with the audience on the main points *and* presents the action you need for them to take.

Again, we have a chapter dedicated to effective closes (see Chapter 6), but for planning, you certainly need to chart a path back to your purpose statement. With this in your presentation plan, even if you get off track at any point, you can return to your purpose statement and refocus for a triumphant closing.

Keep the Time in Mind

Remember the "time cut." While we're still in planning and constructing mode, remember to prepare for a cut in your presentation time. As a salesperson, you know how lucky you are if you end up having thirty minutes with your buyers—even if you're scheduled to have forty-five. Common causes for time cuts are previous presenters going over time, lunch being served too early, and the "big boss" asking to "wrap things up." So you should prepare a tighter version of your plan in case you need to slice 10 to 20 percent off of what you expect to cover before you even begin.

Train yourself to think in shorter "bites." You have expert knowledge of your company's products and services, and you will always be challenged for time because you know far more about them than you have time to explain.

If you don't prepare for a shorter time, you might end up:

- Talking too fast—**wrong!**
- Becoming too flustered to continue—**terrible!**
- Depending on your giant array of slides—**groan!**
- Dropping your powerful close—**no!**

In your planning, separate your topics into units—either with note cards or sticky notes in a prioritized order. While you are rehearsing for time, try alternate order versions, dropping different topics each time to develop your short version. Better to do your own focused trim of ideas than be cut off by some arbitrary clock.

Naked Scenarios

Just as you have learned to organize your thoughts into powerful opening statements, Kyle and Lindsay have learned to do the same. This preparation will not only make their pitches more effective, it will also make them more confident.

Out of the Gate
Working with his coach, Kyle was able to get over his initial presentation fear and focus on selling the Crosswyse products. His coach put him to work creating an opener, purpose statement, and direction for his presentation.

Kyle's Opener
Good afternoon and welcome to each of you. Imagine former president Bill Clinton strolling into your store and asking to buy a bicycle. Remember all those pictures of Clinton out jogging with his secret service agents? Well good ole Bill is in his 60s and, like the 80 or so million other Baby Boomers, he wants to stay active. With the toll age takes on knees and hips, Bill and his Boomer buddies are likely going to trade in their running shoes and switch to bicycles.

Kyle's Purpose Statement
This afternoon you will gain access to a sharp wedge into that market and help you to tap into the trillions of dol-

lars of spending power the fifty- and sixty-something outdoor athletes are carrying.

Lindsay in Action

Lindsay was used to selling her company's services, but
in one-on-one situations. Therefore she not only needed
this confidence-booster session, she also needed to tailor
her materials to a group setting. So, her friend Alexis spent
the next few days after work helping her former roommate
build her confidence—and fight off the cold sweats—when it
came to her group presentation.

Lindsay's Opener

Companies know that *every* minute of downtime impacts
business productivity.

That's why more and more companies today are out-
sourcing to Helpdesk firms. But canceled, unresolved tickets, unreturned phone calls and poorly trained tech support
personnel can create bottlenecks that choke the life out of
your operations ROI.

Lindsay's Purpose Statement

Today, you are going to get a clear idea of how going with
Diamond Helpdesk, Inc. will:

1. Increase contact accountability
2. Reduce response time dramatically—improving productivity. And lastly,
3. Move your helpdesk from being reactive to
   proactive.

The Voyage Home

With the help of planning, a vacation can leave you with a rejuvenated spirit, a great tan, and wonderful memories. The alternative may be itchy mosquito bites, a bad sunburn, and missed opportunities. Thoughtful navigation of your presentations ensures that at the end, both you and your customers will be able to celebrate victoriously with a mission accomplished—a sealed deal!

N-A-K-E-D selling starts with proper *navigation*, which sets forth a plan that takes both parties—salesperson and buyer—into consideration so that a satisfying outcome is created for both.

Chapter 3

KEEP THEM EXCITED

SALES SITUATION: They look like they'd rather be at home in bed. And so would I!

> Can you think of a time when you were offered some food you'd never heard of? Until you know how the creamy richness of crème brûlée both feels and tastes, with the crunchy glazed top crackling on your tongue, you may not be particularly inclined to order it. But once you're convinced, you may excitedly recommend it to others. Perhaps your experience with a new dish was sushi, but again, it was likely a devotee's enthusiasm that finally compelled you to try it.

Initially, customers may be only mildly interested in what you have to offer. You have to issue an invitation that sets up a relationship even before they walk into the room. Even if it's an existing customer relationship, you can think about how this particular presentation could recharge the dynamic between you and them.

How do you open your pitch? Does your opener pull people in immediately? It should. You must lead as enthusiastically as possible, presenting a positive expectation with a wowing opener. You want your enthusiasm for your company's product or service to compel your buyer to try it.

A—Approach the sale and the audience
with enthusiasm.

Get in "the Mood"

Basic psychology tells us that as humans we don't do anything without some kind of motivation. We don't put on a jacket unless it's cold; we don't remember a phone number unless we need it; and we certainly don't sign purchase orders if we aren't enthusiastic about buying. And the bigger the purchase, the more motivated your buyers have to be to *really* want to buy.

> **SalesPEAK Secret:** The bigger the purchase, the more motivated your buyers have to be to *really* want to buy.

Guess what? The buyer sitting there before you didn't wake up this morning saying, "Hey, what a great day to go spend fifty grand of the company's money! I'm excited." Instead, buyers are concerned about everything but that. So it's up to you to create the passion that will drive customer commitment. This means that you have to have at least twice as much passion about your idea or product as usual—and be ready to share it with the customers. Several elements affect the outcome of the presentation:

- Your passion
- Your customer's need and motivation level
- The conditions you create

The sale starts with *you* and your own attitude about your product, your company, your customer, and your presentation.

Your Passion

The audience will respond to the vibe you give off, so a quick "passion check" might be in order as you head out on your sales calls. (Go through the "Passion Quotient" quiz in Appendix A to figure out where your head is as you anticipate this presentation.) Remember, all the content, facts, figures, and solutions in the world won't create a sale if you don't sell with enthusiasm, confidence, and persuasion. Right before you are going to speak, you will need to prepare yourself mentally and physically.

> **SalesPEAK Secret:** Remember, all the content, facts, figures, and solutions in the world won't create a sale if you don't sell with enthusiasm, confidence, and persuasion.

Mentally

You should practice your entire presentation aloud in order to get into the correct frame of mind. You can practice anywhere from in your office before your meeting to in your car while waiting for the light to change. It is important that you feel thoroughly familiar with your material, especially your opener, your purpose statement, transitions, and persuasive close. Remember the card or slide reminders that you built in the preparation stage? These will come in handy.

Also, saying your material out loud in the room where you will be speaking creates anchors that will help you remember your notes. Practice giving your pitch in the conference room where you'll be having your sales call and associate spots in the room with parts of your presentation. Anytime we can combine a visual image with our words, we create a two-sided adhesive that helps ideas stick in our head—so they'll be there when we need them.

Positive performance comes from a combination of preparation and positive expectations. When you can say your presentation aloud, in any order, and feel certain of your recall, then you have a solid reason to expect the best outcome.

Emotionally create a positive expectation. A type of feel-good activity you can do after you arrive (early, of course) is to practice the key parts of your presentation aloud (remember opener, transitions, and power close?) in the room before people come in. While you do this, picture the audience smiling, nodding, and taking notes. Just put the vibe out there and you'll enjoy the feeling when it comes back to you.

Overcoming Your Nerves Is Up to You

Organization in the form of a checklist helps you be mentally prepared as well. When you have confirmed that the projection equipment is set up and working, your handouts are all collated and in folders, and the key decision makers will be attending, then your head is in a good place.

The feeling we call "nervousness" comes from the same adrenalin reaction that causes anticipation. Your body makes the hormone; you perceive whether it's negative (nervousness) or positive (anticipation). The more prepared you are for your pitch, the more stable your mental place, which allows you to be "up" a bit before a presentation, so that you can feel the positive effects of the hormonal reactions.

NAKED TIP: Anxiety is a temporary condition seen and felt by you. Here are some hints and tips on how to reduce your presentation stress.

- Visualize your entire pitch.
- Remind yourself that you're in total control.
- Have your first ninety seconds down cold.
- Practice your closing statement.
- Anticipate questions (more on this in Chapter 5).
- Eat and drink well before your presentation.
- Breathe!

Physically

Being physically prepared is essential to your successful sales experience. Eat and drink well (low sugar, low caffeine, high protein), but not right before you pitch: you need energy at your command, not a full tummy for a nap. Drink only room-temperature beverages, avoiding sugary or carbonated drinks (these cause phlegm, belching, or worse!). Also, avoid eating too many carbohydrates or drinking too much caffeine. You don't need to be bouncing off the walls. High-fat foods will also make you feel sleepy, dull, and bloated.

Next, make sure your adrenaline is up a bit. Excitement will give you the energy to project enthusiasm and infect your audience with it. Transferring energy to the audience may exhaust you by the end of your presentation, but it will increase your effectiveness. You need the adrenaline to project your voice, to move around the room, and to create excitement among the buyers (in addition to all those dramatic gestures that will hold everyone's attention).

This extra power surge will help if your buyers are not as zealous as you are. You'll need that extra juice to captivate and energize the entire room, giving you a leg up on your stiff and dull competition. Remember, you must outsmart, outshine, and out-market those who are also vying for the same deal.

SalesPEAK Secret: Remember, you must outsmart, outshine, and out-market those who are also vying for the same deal.

Fidgeting Isn't Always a Bad Thing

What if you find yourself fidgeting? Fidgeting is the body's way of getting the brain to release endorphins—that "feel good" chemical that athletes enjoy as the "runner's high." You can accomplish positive fidgeting by squeezing a stress ball or even dancing (before the customers come into the room, of course). A little stretching could also do you some good. Just remember to organize your appearance if you stretch while in your speaking clothes.

If fidgeting comes through in your legs, as in pacing or rocking, make sure you jump up and down, or run in place somewhere (not in front of the audience, of course). This will get the blood flowing in a positive way—toward your brain—instead of toward your feet.

NAKED TIP: For a confident, relaxed delivery, take these suggestions:

Laugh—opens vocal chords, makes you feel good.

Breathe Deeply—gets oxygen to brain, helps you think clearly; also lowers heart rate.

Reframe—avoid any negative words— change "nervousness" to "energy," change "fidgeting" to "powering up."

Voice Management—relax vocal chords with warmups: *Aaahhh, uuuhhhmmm.*

Move—channels energy and keeps you close to decision-makers.

The Buyer's Motivation

While you've spent all this time getting ready for your presentation, preparing your materials, and getting into a prepared mental state, your buyer has been going along his day, doing a million different things, not really concentrating on your upcoming pitch. Therefore, when he walks into the conference room it's your job to make your product his sole priority. Here are three suggestions on how to make this happen.

#1. Play Music as Everyone Comes into the Presentation Area

They've been at their desks all day; help them shift their gears and their expectations by having feel-good music to set the tone. If you want high energy, don't play classical. Bring in some upbeat rock or some jazz. Use music congruent with the audience, the message, the time of day, and the theme of the meeting. Think about your message as well as your audience's age. In other words, I wouldn't play Motown for a group of twenty-two-year-olds; likewise, I wouldn't put rap on for fifty-year-olds!

#2. Connect Personally with Everyone Who Enters the Room

This will help you be a better presenter who is more at ease with your audience. If there's time beforehand, greet people, shake hands, schmooze, and build initial relationships with decision makers and their advisors. Gather the names of those people you will be presenting to so that you can address them by name during your pitch. This will make those people feel very connected and encourage your own sense of connection to the group. If there isn't time beforehand, though, do not spend the first few minutes of your presentation working your way up to the front chatting with people, as we warned against earlier.

SalesPEAK Secret: Try and gather the names of those people you will be presenting to so that you can address them by name during your pitch.

#3. Keep the Lights *On* During the Presentation—the Brighter the Room, the Higher the Energy

Even if you're using a digital slideshow, leaving lights *up* creates a brighter mood! Open the shades, or if there are no windows, ask for added lamps to generate more light in a dark conference room. You want the customers awake and listening, not daydreaming under the assumption it's a good time for a snooze.

Seating Strategy

To be persuasive and influential with your customers, you will want to plan where people will sit without being too forced or formal about it. Obviously you can't control seating in advance all the time, especially when you are going to a customer's site. There are occasions, though, when you can work a seating strategy to your advantage.

For example, if you happen to be presenting to a group in a conference room but have a few of your own team members present, you can place yourself and your team at random spots in order to mix in with the buyers. You wouldn't want all of your customers sitting on one side of the room, while you and your colleagues are on the other. That's way too combative.

NAKED TIP: If, after arriving early, you find yourself at a conference table, place your binder, briefcase, and other belongings down on the table. When people arrive and are beginning to take their seats, move to the most strategic spot like you had intended to sit there all along.

Seating arrangements always have a strategic implication because naked personal space and territory are always a factor.

Found Arrangements

Here are some examples of not-so-helpful seating designs, with strategies to help them work to your benefit. These are some typical setups you might find when you arrive, as well as some you can create when you have freedom to arrange seating.

The T Setup

This is when the audience is all sitting on one side of Table A, which is running horizontally, and Table B is running perpendicular to Table A as a buffer between the salesperson and the audience.

The T is an "ambush" setup, definitely combative, or at the least defensive. The ones at the back table want to keep their distance and maintain a power position. Sitting nearer to you will either be your ally (the one who is already sold or who stands to benefit from your product or service) or the sniper (the one who will try to catch you off-guard).

The Solution

Avoid standing or sitting in the designated "hot spot" at the end of Table B. Strategic management would be to move your setup to the right of Table B, so that the listeners would have to sit at both Table A and Table B in order to face you, creating a semicircle. You can set up an easel with a flip chart or whiteboard there to stake your claim to that space. Move around the room to use your personal power to get past their seating-plan defenses.

The U Setup

The U Setup is when three or more tables are put together in a U shape, with the audience sitting on the outside of the tables and the salesperson expected to stand at the mouth of the U.

The U is the least advantageous arrangement for you for two reasons; it limits your ability to move around, and it creates a sort of gauntlet or box canyon effect. Decision makers are on the outside, and you are trapped on the inside. It is very easy for them to take shots at you from their protected outer perimeter. You won't be able to stand close to decision makers (who often seem to sit at the back) because it would involve turning your back to the ones closer to you.

Because people feel protected behind their "walls," they are not only likely to disagree but also to riddle you with sniper bullets. It's also too easy for them to have side conversations, send text messages from under the table, and even doodle. In any case, you won't be able to take charge of the buyers' attention.

The Solution

Walking around to the outside of the tables is a better bet; however, you are still a long way away from those on the other side of the room.

Another idea is to move the chairs to the inside of the U with each one facing the opening of the U. This arrangement brings everyone closer together and no one is blocked behind the table. You get a better connection and can keep everyone's attention more effectively.

If you decide to sit after the chairs are moved, sit in the center. This puts you on a more equal setting and in closer proximity to the decision makers, though it may be a bit crowded.

A better solution is to arrive early and move the tables if they aren't bolted to the floor. Just get permission from someone at the office. You can always put them back when you are done with your presentation.

Naked Arrangements

The very core of the *Naked Salesperson* approach is true and unrestricted human connection. Just changing seating configuration can move you closer to achieving that. More personal is more effective. Your enthusiasm can really come through when the customers are around you in a positive arrangement. The closer you are to the customer, without invading personal space, the better able you are to influence that person on an individual level.

NAKED TIP: The Law of *Oxyproxism*: The closer, physically, you are to the audience members, the more influential you can be in your talk.

Naked arrangements encourage positive interaction. Remember the Knights of the Round Table? Circle configurations, for example, create harmony. But since you have to be thoroughly visible to all (as the center of attention), you will want to use a variation of the circle. Have people sit together in semicircles, team style (all facing front, round tables) when there are fifteen plus.

Another desirable setup is the herringbone—or classroom style—where tables are split into two rows and angled in with everyone facing forward, focused on you. You are visually accessible to the customers, and they are close to you for best personal-space relations. Now that the lighting is right and everyone is all cozy and seated, you have your one chance to really grab their attention.

SalesPEAK Secret: More personal is more effective. Your enthusiasm can really come through when the customers are around you in a positive arrangement.

The Taste Test

Back to the example of the sushi. . . . You may take that first bite based on someone's enthusiastic recommendation or even subtle coercion (like a dare), but if it's not pleasing to your palate, you'll probably order the hibachi steak instead. Your buyers are no different.

Have you ever heard of the "halo effect"? It's pretty much the principle of first impressions. Just as a job interviewer makes his or her decision in the first sixty seconds or so, your audience will do the same. Remember, we relate to each other's nakedness—people to people. That first taste, if prepared and executed properly, will carry you through the meal, and have them back ordering more. If it doesn't, your customers will be ordering the hibachi steak from your competitor.

Chapter 2 introduced you to many dos and don'ts of opening a presentation, but let's play out some of those suggested scenarios here:

Salesperson One: Chatting to folks in asides on his way to the front of the room, he smiles a sort of strained half-smile, rubs his hands together and says, "Okay, we've got a lot to cover today; let's get started. My name is Harry Halfwit and I'm here to talk to you today about my company and this great product you really should buy."

Salesperson Two: "Hi guys, how is everybody today? You doin' okay?" She shuffles her notes a bit as she looks down, then turns to the slide that is up on the screen. "Can everybody see what's up here? Can everybody see me? Well, all right!"

Harry's opening is as appealing as a bran muffin and Salesperson Two's presentation is as appetizing as a bucket of fish heads. Neither salesperson has adopted the approach of selling naked, and therefore both will ultimately fail in securing a buy from their customers. Between Harry's unprofessional chitchatting and Number Two's lack of preparation and confidence, it would be a shock if anyone paid attention through to the end of their pitches.

Let's take a look at how a real naked salesperson would handle his opening . . .

NAKED SALESPERSON STUDY: Anson

A member of the customer's group who is favorably disposed to the product introduces him. "This is Anson Plyler with XYZ Corporation who's going to help us cut operations costs."

Anson steps up to the center of the speaking area (what we call the power spot), pauses briefly with a strong but relaxed speaker's stance, then says, "Your company currently leads the market in new customer growth. But projections from Hickory Dickery research firm show a strong shift in product delivery expectations. You guys are the big dogs now, but your 42,000 customers will soon be expecting two-day turnaround instead of the four you have now. (Pause) To get ahead, you are going to have to cut order-to-delivery time in half. We can make that happen for you."

The customer thinks: "Wow! Someone who didn't start with 'me, me and my company and me some more.' Someone who told me something I hadn't heard that affects my business directly. Someone who sounds like he gets where we're coming from. I'd like a piece of that."

Now that's crème brûlée!

The old speaker's adage couldn't be truer in selling presentations: They don't care how much you know until they know how much you care.

> **SalesPEAK Secret:** They don't care how much you know until they know how much you care.

An opening that sets the customer up as the star creates a "halo effect" for what you will have to say throughout the rest of your presentation. On the other hand, an opening that sounds cliché and familiar while it points the spotlight on you suggests a very dull time. You will be able to see the boredom on every customer's face. As mentioned earlier, you need an opening that really resonates with the crowd and draws them in so that they are interested in your pitch from the start.

Three great tools to use when putting together a stellar opening are statistics, props, and stories. Let's take a closer look to see how each can be utilized in your opening.

The Numbers Don't Lie

In the Naked Salesperson Study above, the speaker shared statistics from a reliable source that would relate directly to the customer's situation. Be sure the statistics tie directly to the customer's business. Using stats just to show you can do research is borderline offensive to listeners.

Break Out the Toys

A speaker, holding up an inflated ball, begins to bounce it on the floor as he speaks, "Bottom out, bounce up, bottom out, bounce up, bottom out . . ." He pauses. "Wouldn't it be nice to eliminate that seasonal dip that your company has to plan around every year? The hiring, the layoffs, the hiring, then in a few months more layoffs. Our personnel management program can help you shoot straight to profits." Then he passes the ball quickly to a decision maker (who, of course, gets to keep the ball).

That opening is compelling because it is visually engaging, comparing an actual bouncing ball to the company's rising and falling sales scenarios, and it catches the direct attention of the decision maker.

Props are fun for you, help you stay on track, and draw the audience in. Use them to demonstrate or compare to some element of the company's need or some benefit of your product. Be as creative as you like, but be sure to explain the comparison; don't leave it to the customers to figure out.

Be warned, though. Some prop openings sound better in our own heads than in practice, so test the concept out on a colleague first.

Spin a Great Story

Stories offer another element that invites attention, but as openers they need to be relevant. This is why jokes or random stories drawn from some generic speaker's source-book can tarnish that halo.

You want to make sure the story you choose to tell grabs the buyer's attention, is relevant or relatable to his current situation, and excites him with promised greatness—if he purchases your company's product or service. For example, take the following story opener:

> An Olympic speed skater in an elimination heat fell at the very end of the race within feet of the finish line, apparently tripped by another skater. He could have screamed "foul" or had a frustration tantrum right there. Instead, he rose to his knees and crawled across the finish line. You see, he knew that as long as he placed in the competition, he would qualify for the final round. By self-discipline, restraint, and clear thinking, he moved on and ultimately won the gold.
>
> Your company has been tripped up by the new government regulations. But with the operations changes provided by our service and your own self-discipline, restraint, and clear thinking, you can still grab the gold! Now . . .

Whether you use statistics, a prop, a story, a startling fact, or some other attention-getting opener, remember that with the right enticement, even the doubter will try the sushi.

With so many effective ways to open, one way *not* to open your presentation is to give out mountains of paper or to talk about your headquarters location. Boring! This is a good place to discuss handouts and the way they support your strategy.

SalesPEAK Secret: With so many effective ways to open, one way *not* to open your presentation is to give out mountains of paper or to talk about your headquarters location.

Handouts

With your "day of" checklist and your advanced preparation completed weeks before, you have likely anticipated what paper backup you will need.

For your "bottom-line" person—a detailed IT manager, a human resources VP, and other analytical executives—you might have return-on-investment projections and feasibility or facilities assessments. For a purchasing manager, you will likely need to have price and features comparisons to the competition. In addition, you can add product reviews, awards your company has won, and recent press releases. Finally, you should also bring a printed version of any slides that you use during your presentation.

Whatever you bring from your company, your best bet is to customize the handouts for that particular customer. It's easy enough to include their company's name on your presentation materials, and it makes it seem like this isn't just a stock pitch. Bring these backup documents in a separate folder so that they are easily accessible when it's time to hand them out. Or, better yet, have the packets or collated copies individually prepared and labeled for each person who is at your presentation.

Hand Out Before or After?

Avoid handing them out at the beginning. One reason you do not want to hand out the packets of information (or your complete printed-out slide presentation) before you begin your pitch is that the buyer is inclined to flip through the pages and just tune you out. After all, why bother listening if the handout packet is provided?

To combat this possible turn of events, at the end of your presentation, ask if anyone would like the handouts and/or a copy of your presentation. Believe me, those who hate paper won't take them, and those who want more information will tip their chairs over to grab the information that you have.

If packets sold products, presentations wouldn't be necessary. However, naked customers buy from naked sellers, not from paper. Your presentation is more than the paper it's printed on. Even if you do decide to use handouts, you need to put together a presentation that is certain to wow.

> **SalesPEAK Secret:** Your presentation is more than the paper it's printed on.

Organize for Your Buyers

If you do decide to put together handouts for your presentation, or if you are bringing the actual proposal for authorization, provide someplace for the customers to *put* their information. A folder or envelope of some kind helps your customers stay organized. Keep in mind that when the customers leave your presentation, they'll be going to other meetings with more papers. Help them keep your material together so that they can easily refer to your presentation. If it's all in one place, it's easier for them to recall your presentation as a whole.

While we are on the discussion of paper and handouts, what color is most paper? Yes, it's white. What color are your handouts? What is the color of your folder? If everything you give your clients is white, you can expect them to lose it in the sea of paper floating around their offices. Give them a *green* folder (or some other color), with green handouts, or use their company colors as your accent colors so that they are more likely to find and remember your handouts. You want all your information to be as accessible to the buyer as possible—even after your presentation is over. Putting together a handout that really *stands* out will help your buyer remember your product.

THE HANDOUTS RULES

Rule #1: Don't give out the info packet as part of your opener.

Rule #2: Help customers organize and retain your handouts to support their decisions.

Rule #3: Do something different to be remembered.

> **SalesPEAK** Secret: Putting together a handout that really *stands* out will help your buyer remember your pitch.

Naked Scenarios

Both Kyle and Lindsay learned how to incorporate various elements into their pitches in order to keep the attention of the different types of listeners—just like you did. Let's see how they put this information to use in their pitches.

Kyle's Big Day

Kyle's colleague, Brian, walked into the presentation room catching Kyle at the front of the room sitting on the Cross-Trick bike. He had his arms resting on the handlebars, head down, feet on the floor pushing the bike forward and back.

"Hey man. Snap out of it. We've got five buyers and some of their store people coming in here in less than three hours. What are you doing?"

Kyle looked up. "Brian, we're up against the big boys on this with their huge expense accounts and hospitality suites. It's gonna take something pretty spectacular to get their attention. My coach says that 'you have to open with re-direction.'"

"With, uh . . . what?"

"Redirection. They're not coming in here thinking about us, or what we can do for them. We've got to go out and grab 'em some sort of way . . . and I don't know if I'm up to it." Kyle shook his head. "Can't you just do this?"

"Okay, Kyle. Let's focus here. We're at a trade show with 250 other companies, but I've managed to get some big-money people to agree to attend your presentation. I know I'm magic at the mic, but they want to hear the designer—the guy who's baby this is." He paused to make sure Kyle was following. "You have the passion about these bikes and what they do. I mean you're the one who came up with the idea of promoting bikes to corporations with multiple campuses for employees—the whole "green" thing. That's brilliant!"

Kyle responded flatly, "Maybe, but today is still going to be tough." He rolled on the bike slowly, then threw a bar-spin and bounced up into a tail-whip.

Brian glanced over at Kyle's BMX flatland stunts on the prototype trick bike. Suddenly, he blurted, "That's it!"

Kyle's eyes brightened as Brian's idea hit him without Brian even having to say it. "Yeah! We can set up a small ramp; this room's big enough."

"Call that kid you know, the one that you guys did that show with."

"Deven? Sure. He can do some simple air stuff and a little flatland." His words quickened. "And we've got some samples of our new sprocket we can put in front of each of them, you know, for the 'haptic' ones."

"The *what* ones? "

"The haptic ones—it's a type of audience member my presentation coach taught me about. She says those types of listeners respond best to demos and product samples. If they're able to touch it, they'll listen more intently."

"Yeah, we can tie the opening stunts into the slides. It'll be great . . ." Brian continued.

* * *

At 4 P.M. the buyers began to drift into the room. Brian was at the door, shaking hands with the customers as they came in. "Hey Steven, come on in, who's that you have with you? Oh is that your corporate sales guy? You need to meet our designer, Kyle. Come on over here. We've got a great presentation for you today."

At 4:15 everyone moved to the tables set up in a semi-circle with the chairs all placed on the backside of the tables and facing the front. Suddenly, what looked like fog began to drift into the room; a strobe light flashed and a twelve-year-old boy came out riding the Crosswyse CrossTrick bike, launching into the air with a back flip off the ramp, landing perfectly in front of the audience.

All chatting and fidgeting stopped; every person in the audience (and even a few looking in from outside the room) came to attention. Kyle had succeeded in creating an attention-getting opener.

"You've just witnessed a new sensation in bikes—the Crosswyse CrossTrick. Paired with the Crosswyse Cross-Trainer, they are the new bikes for active riders—of any age."

All went well for the introduction and the first two topics, but about fifteen minutes into the presentation Kyle noticed that a few people were starting to shift and fidget. He stopped his technical piece mid-sentence.

" . . . and the principle behind . . . You know, we need to stop and shift gears here for a minute. Instead of listening to me talk about the structural integrity of these bikes, why don't you reach under your seat where you'll find our patented sprocket. Turn it over in your hands and feel the trueness of the cuts and the surfaces. This is the kind of uniqueness in quality control and performance you will be able to expect from the Crosswyse line."

The audience members took the sprockets out and studied them. They nodded and commented to each other as they rubbed the gleaming parts—all faces looking pleased and positive. Kyle cut an eye over to Brian who gave him a thumbs-up.

Lindsay in Action

Lindsay paced her office, shuffling the notes in her hands as she read them aloud during her practice run-through.

" . . . and the second problem you guys have . . ." she said in her professional voice as she gestured with the papers. But then she stopped and added in a mumble, "No, that's negative. We don't want to say that they aren't running their business well. That's shooting ourselves in the foot." She chewed for a second on the pencil in her other hand. ". . .and the next reason to consider . . ." She stopped again. "That's not strong enough . . ." Erasing a couple lines on the notes, scribbling some new text, Lindsay began again.

". . .and the next contribution that our company's help-desk services can make to your bottom line is . . ."

"Yeah, now you're getting there." Lindsay's manager Michelle had been eavesdropping. "How's it going?"

"Okay, maybe. I can get the words right, I think . . . I mean it's what I do every day with my sales calls. But that's only one person. How can I get all these people to hang with me through all the numbers—the unclosed tickets, the callbacks, the unresolved requests? That's a lot of data, but it's our best shot at hard proof that we really are the best." Lindsay looked down at her notes, a puzzled expression on her face.

"Okay, well what about your friend, that sales coach? Didn't she say that you could use stuff to keep their attention? Weren't you telling me about props and other stuff?"

"You're right—I could use some props. That'll keep them occupied. Thanks Michelle."

"*Ah*, just another job well done. So many people to enlighten; so little time . . . " Michelle gave a little laugh as she ducked back out of Lindsay's office, leaving her to prepare.

* * *

"Now, let's review the performance data." Lindsay was using body language and movement around the conference table to keep everyone focused, but she could see them beginning to move restlessly in their chairs. "Ray, would you be kind enough to hand out these quality analysis sheets?" She gave the customer sitting closest to her the pale green data sheets. "And, Christina, can you give everyone a piece of this gum?" She handed her a pack of gum to pass around.

After both were distributed to all eight in the audience, Lindsay started her prop-propelled pitch. "Thanks guys. Now, if you would, open the gum and chew it." As several people smiled while they unfolded the gum's wrapper and put it the piece in their mouths, Lindsay walked over to a senior operations manager and handed him one more piece. "How about another?" She continued, "What if I gave you four more pieces every thirty minutes?" She counted out four more pieces and laid those in front of him as well. "That's about the rate that your company's employees call into your helpdesk."

The manager looked around a little nervously, but was a good sport and unwrapped another piece, pretending to have his mouth full, which produced a little chuckling.

"Maybe you can handle more pieces of gum by spitting the old pieces out. Or, if the end of the day comes and you haven't chewed it all, what do you do? Just throw away the ones you didn't get to?"

She continued as people were chewing their gum and beginning to look over the data sheets. "Your current offshore helpdesk does just this. If you look at Column 3—note the number of unresolved tickets you've had each day. Whose ticket is more important? Whose gets dropped at the end of the day?"

She paused to give them five seconds to look over the data sheet before she called them back to focus on her. "Now look at the last column on the right. That is the number of unresolved helpdesk tickets *our* system can eliminate for you. With our company, you can expect fewer than *three* in the day they are called in and *zero* that are not followed up on within twenty-four hours."

Lindsay stopped and watched them as they read over the quality analysis comparison. Many were nodding favorably. Finally, the operations manager raised his hand, "Hey, I see your point, but now what am I supposed to do with all this gum?"

The group laughed and Lindsay let out a confident breath.

The Mirror

Ultimately, the buyer's reaction will mirror what she sees in you. You need to look like you are having a good time, are truly credible, and are enthusiastically convinced that you are in fact offering her a solution to her problems. You've heard the expression, "what you see is what you get," right? Well, what customers see is what they will give back to you. They care about their own business and about how you are going to handle the time they've allotted to you.

Arrive at your presentation N-A-K-E-D and ready to *approach* your buyers with enthusiasm—solid in your knowledge, passionate in your commitment, and confident of your ability to connect with the decision makers. This will make you the dealmaker.

Chapter 4

PULL THEM IN

SALES SITUATION: They're not listening; how do I pull them in?

You've sweated many long hours to put together your presentation. You've managed to secure commitments from buyers at the senior level to sit in. You set up the room early so everything would run smoothly. Your opener went great and you're really on a roll. And then, after a few minutes, you turn and notice that one person has his head down and is playing with his iPhone. Another is looking at you, but it's like she's looking through you, thinking about a million other things. The senior buyer has his arms crossed over his chest, taking quick glances at his watch. In short, the lights are on but nobody's home in your audience.

Your neck begins to redden; perspiration beads on your brow, and you begin talking faster, thinking, "Maybe if I hurry up, they'll pay attention."

STOP!

Do you *really* think boring them at a higher speed will help?

Naked salespeople know that everyone in the room must feel like:

- They are having a conversation directly with you.
- You are intuitively answering all of their questions and hitting the important points.

Otherwise, no sale.

And this is what makes our mouths go dry and our brains check out in the middle of the presentation. So, let's learn how *not* to lose their attention and how to be sure to make a striking impression *every* time.

K—Keep the audience with you throughout
your presentation.

Attention Competition

When you are doing a sales presentation—actually, anytime you are speaking to a group and asking for action from them—you are not only competing with other products in the same category, you are competing with your listeners' random thoughts.

Think about the idea of naked selling: a genuine exchange, a mental transaction, between two humans. You need to connect with your audience on a very basic, stripped-down level in order to succeed in your sale. All too often this ideal exchange doesn't occur; sometimes our listeners just fade away.

SalesPEAK Secret: You need to connect with your audience on a very basic, stripped-down level in order to succeed in your sale.

Sometimes you cannot prevent this failure to listen. Once in a while you will run into someone who just does not have an attention span. However, those cases are rare. Most often, buyers do not pay attention because the salesperson is doing something wrong. Here's what usually happens in those situations:

1. The speaker is only talking about himself or his company.
2. The speaker is incessant—droning on and on without a break.
3. The speaker is talking in a monotone—*boring*!
4. What is being said has no direct relevance to the buyers.
5. The audience doesn't understand the language or terminology the speaker is using.
6. The buyers feel disconnected from the "human" on the other side of the conversation—like they're not receiving the speaker's attention.

You have to work for your buyer's attention. Get over yourself and focus your energy on the real star of the day—the buyers.

Once you can accomplish a successful style of communication by avoiding the pitfalls listed above, you will be successful in all conversation, whether you are selling your company's products and services to a group, your skills to a panel of prospective employers, or your charms to a potential date. This chapter will give you that edge (but we will only be focusing on sales presentations—charming dates is another book!).

Don't Just Stand There, *Stand There!*

Your stance—where you stand, how you stand, and what you vary about your stance while you are speaking—is a core element to successfully managing the audience's attention. You want to command a presence as soon as you step into the room and take your spot. When you enter the room where you'll be pitching:

- Remain standing.
- Locate your "power place."
- Relax your hands at your sides.
- Stand with feet a shoulder's width apart for stability.
- Lift your sternum (the bone in the center of your chest where your ribs hook together).
- Use your body to emphasize points.

Creating the proper stance for your pitch gives you the appearance of calm confidence and inspires trust. It is also a commanding position, which draws the audience's attention. Let's break each step down so you know how to accomplish a powerful stance during your next presentation.

SalesPEAK Secret: Your stance—where you stand, how you stand, and what you vary about your stance while you are speaking— is a core element to successfully managing the audience's attention.

Stay Standing

If presenting for a group of buyers, you will be more effective standing naked instead of sitting naked. This is especially true when you are in a small meeting situation where everyone is sitting. If you stand to speak, you take a power position and command everyone's attention. (This is especially helpful if you are short.)

Find Your Power Place

When you enter the room where you'll be presenting, locate a "power place." This is where you can begin speaking from and return to regularly during your presentation. Having a particular spot that you return to over and over again during your pitch helps to emphasize a certain statement, show a change in direction, or transition between points.

Handle Your Hands

Hands relaxed at our sides? We rarely seem to be able to do that even in conversation, let alone in front of a group. We put them in our pockets, hold a pen, hold a glass, clasp them together, and even drum our fingers on a table. But you must remember: you should be helping the audience to feel at ease, not making them more nervous. They should be confident in your credibility and professional value to them. If they find *you* credible, they will find your *information* and your *action recommendations* credible. A relaxed stance with your hands comfortably by your sides conveys confidence and believability.

> **SalesPEAK Secret:** A relaxed stance with your hands comfortably by your sides conveys confidence and believability.

Here's what to avoid when you're standing up in front of the group and making your pitch:

No hands in your pockets (what are you doing in there?)

No clasped or folded hands (says, "I can't wait until this is over")

No hands behind back (are you in military "at ease"?)

No "fig-leaf pose" with your hands in front of your privates (nothing nonverbally says "I feel uncomfortably exposed" like your hands over your crotch)

The reason that keeping our hands at our sides is an uncomfortable stance for us is that we feel vulnerable and unprotected. That's perfect! When you relax your guarded position (hands up or across your body in a protective stance), you open up and invite the audience in to your presentation. If you are observably at ease in a vulnerable position, then they see you as supremely confident in what you are saying. *And* they will trust you. You want to show to your buyers that you are *comfortable* with being exposed—you have nothing to hide.

> **SalesPEAK** Secret: You want to show to your buyers that you are *comfortable* with being exposed—you have nothing to hide.

Lean In

You can engage listeners with your stance just by varying it a bit. When making a point, lean in slightly while you speak to pull listeners into what you are saying, then straighten back up to draw them to you. Leaning in from the waist allows you to make more effective eye contact with decision makers. If the group is large, leaning in puts you at eye level. It also makes you look more welcoming and engaged with the group.

Our stance, upright or leaning in, sends very specific messages to our audiences. If we hunch or stand with hands or arms crossed in front of us, we are saying, "Stay away!" But if we are upright and lean closer to them in a welcoming way, we invite the audience to be involved with our ideas.

NAKED TIP: Stand proud during your presentation. Good posture is a sign of confidence, and a confident salesperson is a successful salesperson. You should:

- Avoid leaning on podium or wall
- Have feet about shoulder width apart
- Control your hands

Move It Out!

Whenever you break your stance and move from your power spot, move deliberately. Step toward one side of the room to gain attention with your physical presence. After a few slow steps, while you continue to talk, stop and resume your speaker's stance.

> **SalesPEAK** Secret: Whenever you break your stance and move from your power spot, move deliberately.

Here are some suggestions on how to use deliberate movement to your advantage.

Get Close, Stay Connected

Moving close to one side of the room or walking out into the audience and standing close to someone while you talk are ways of using your personal presence to engage audience members. Be careful, though, not to crowd anyone— personal space is the comfort circle each of us defines that we don't want others to invade. If you move too close, you might be viewed as attempting dominance: not a good ploy with a buyer. You should never shove a microphone into someone's face either, for the same reason.

Any time you move toward someone specifically, it should be for a positive connection: to answer a question or to hand her a sales sample to study or comment on. When you move beyond your power place, you open yourself to your audience. They recognize this naked gesture and respond with their attention.

Think for a moment about a shorter person who never leaves her seat, or a shy salesperson who stands far away from his presentation group in order to stay protected. These types of salespeople are jeopardizing their sale. When you are accountable for results from a sales pitch, your job is to go out and connect with the audience, not expect them to come and connect with you. Getting out and into the group enhances the connection and will better your buy.

SalesPEAK Secret: When you are accountable for results from a sales pitch, your job is to go out and connect with the audience, not expect them to come and connect with you.

Spread the Wealth

Stay close to your people to keep their attention, but make sure to walk among all of them. Move to the back and around the room, but avoid speaking from the back of the room—a faceless voice isn't as effective for us mortals as it is for deities.

Practice walking while you speak. Your brain works differently when you are standing and walking than when you're sitting. Again, be sure to get up to rehearse. You don't want to trip over your words, or worse—your feet.

NAKED TIP: Avoid crepe-soled shoes. They can make you trip on carpet. Women, no high heels—if you totter, you lose that relaxed, competent air.

And Return

Walk back to your power place for major points in your pitch, especially the conclusion. If you've been out among the group of buyers, they will follow you as you return to the front, and you will have their complete focus for your final remarks.

Body Talk—Work It!

We've looked at stance and movement, now let's go to the real power: gestures and facial expression.

An effective sales pitch is like *charades with words*. Are you familiar with the game of charades? If not, it's a party game that has people take turns gesturing and acting out motions in an attempt to get others to guess a famous name, movie, television show, or phrase—without words. Perhaps the amusement of this game escapes you, until you think of someone like your boss acting out a chicken laying an egg. The scratching, arms flapping like wings, face red from straining . . . got the visual now?

Even though no words or sounds are allowed, the other people in the group almost always end up guessing what the person is acting out. Keep this in mind when you build your presentation. Punctuate your most important points with hand gestures and body movements. Your audiences will not only hear you, they will also see and understand. This will lead to the embrace: when they hear, see, and feel you, they will embrace your product or service and commit to it when you get to the close.

> **SalesPEAK Secret:** Punctuate your most important points with hand gestures and body movements.

Here's some further explanation on how you can make the most out of getting out there and moving around.

Hand Gestures

We communicate all the time, in every mannerism, expression, dip of an eyebrow, movement of a hand. For most of us, though, this is involuntary. Our gestures just sort of happen. However, naked salespeople understand the meaning of different hand movements and how these gestures can help get a point across during their pitch. Deliberate use of hand gestures to support, substitute for, or emphasize words and phrases will amplify your message. Used strategically, hand gestures can take the place of props and many other presentation aids. You need to understand how they can help, though, before you go waving your arms about during your next pitch.

Get Them to See What You're Thinking

Help your audience to visualize what you are saying. When you are at the front of a big room, the listeners need multiple cues to really get the importance of your message. Using your hands and gesturing creates a visual that reinforces your words. Hand gestures also make you appear larger and easier to see by those in the back of the room.

Think of this technique as a running mime routine, much like you would use to communicate if you were in a foreign country and didn't speak the language.

So, if you are talking about a *big* sale, don't use a small gesture—make it a *big*, sweeping movement! If you are talking about someone signing a check, mime that action when you deliver your line. As the old saying goes, "seeing is believing."

> **SalesPEAK Secret:** Using your hands and gesturing creates a visual that reinforces your words.

Give Yourself a Helping Hand

Another important use for your hands is help out your own thinking process. According to David MacNeill from the MacNeill Gesture Lab at the University of Chicago's Department of Linguistics, we use gestures to communicate along with and sometimes in place of words. For example, have you ever watched someone talking on a cell phone, but still using their hands to punctuate what they are saying?

Test it out yourself. Think of the phrase, "It's over there." Now pretend you're directing someone with that line. Can you say it without pointing to where "it" is?

MacNeill further suggests that gesturing also stimulates our brain to use more vivid language. Moving our hands in a communicative way helps organize our thoughts and allows us to retrieve them more easily. So, using your hands to illustrate what you are saying also stimulates your thinking and makes your presentation go better.

Avoid Being **Too** Handy

As you begin using your hands more freely in speaking to punctuate what you're saying, be careful to avoid pointing at people with your finger. That is considered threatening and aggressive. If you must point to someone or something during your presentation, use your entire hand, all fingers extended and touching. (Practice this movement, as it's not a natural movement, but it is much more effective than using your finger or a pen to point.)

Another caution, when it comes to using gestures during your pitch, avoid being overly repetitious. If you use your hands naturally when you talk, you may get into a predictable rhythm, like a conductor leading an orchestra. Be sure to vary your hand movements.

SalesPEAK Secret: If you must point to someone or something during your presentation, use your entire hand, all fingers extended and touching.

Be careful not to overthink the use of gestures, or avoid them all together. Not using your hands is a signal as well. If you keep your hands clasped together or hidden, you convey shiftiness. Audiences will wonder what you are hiding and may become suspicious of your credibility or your motives.

GOOD HAND USE
- Emphasizing a particular point
- Miming a necessary action
- Directing the audience's attention

BAD HAND USE
- Pointing directly at one particular person
- Becoming repetitious in your movements
- Not using your hands at all

Face Up to the Audience

Facial expressions can also punctuate what you're saying. In conversation you smile when you think of something positive, raise your eyebrows when surprised, grimace when you become frightened, and frown when you hear something sad. Why not utilize those types of facial expressions when you are making your pitch? Facial expressions help you to communicate when you are conversing; they can also help you to convince buyers when you are selling.

> **SalesPEAK** Secret: Facial expressions help you to communicate when you are conversing; they can also help you to convince buyers when you are selling.

Faces go flat when we are under stress, so it makes sense to overemphasize expressions occasionally to bring them to a normal level. Looking stiff suggests irritation or negativity. So smile! Your audience will pay attention if you smile at them regularly.

They Are Watching You

As adults we learn to monitor facial expression. We think about what we're going to say based on how a person is looking. We try to judge a reaction by their facial expressions. And we are always attempting to decipher an expressionless "poker face." Therefore, you should be aware that your buyers are watching your every curl of your lip, raise of your brow, and crinkle of your nose. There's no reason that you can't summon up a pleasant look for your presentation.

> **SalesPEAK Secret:** Be aware that your buyers are watching your every curl of your lip, raise of your brow, and crinkle of your nose.

As you have read many times throughout this book, your buyers don't know what's going on inside you at the moment of your pitch. They can't tell if you're nervous, or tired, or sick. They only know what they can see, and you need them to see you as a confident, knowledgeable salesperson in order to secure the buy.

However, your expressions must match what you're saying. Don't smile when you are telling a gut-wrenching story, and don't frown when you are reporting positive test results. Also, saying, for instance, that installation of your product is easy when you don't believe it is so is not going to be helped by having a fake smile plastered on your face. Your buyers know what a real smile looks like—crinkling up the face, wrinkling the nose, lowering the eyebrows, squinting the eyes a bit at the corners. If you aren't really smiling, your audience isn't going to buy it—or buy what you're saying.

When someone responds to a question, a supportive smile and nod from you will invite others to participate. When you genuinely express your enthusiasm, sincerity, concern, joy, or awe, your audience will feel it and connect with your conviction. Naked sales presentations are about inspiring the audience using these types of human connections.

Frankly, though, it doesn't hurt to practice the expressions you want to use in front of a mirror. Your audience will respond more positively to you if you look like you are enjoying yourself. If you rehearse and perfect your enthusiastic "presenter's face" and believe in your presentation, it won't matter how you're really feeling that day.

Eyes Front!

If listeners see an expressionless face or averted eyes instead of enthusiasm and solid eye contact, they will view you as unfriendly or lacking confidence in your product or idea. Forget all those old adages like "speak to the wall behind everyone" or "look over everyone's heads." Speak to the wall? Come on, you will feel weird, everyone in the audience will feel alienated, and you won't have a clue how your presentation is going over. (Oh, and about that other old saying, definitely do *not* picture your audience in their underwear. That could distract you from your topic and cause you to come to a dead stop in the middle of a sentence!)

> **SalesPEAK Secret:** Forget all those old adages like "speak to the wall behind everyone" or "look over everyone's heads."

Instead, look at your audience. How are they reacting to what you are saying? *Are* they reacting? Nodding in agreement? Leaning forward in interest? Or are they glazed over, puzzled by the terms you are using, unclear about the point you are trying to make?

NAKED TIP: Occasionally, you might have to pull an audience member away from the e-mail he is typing on his Black-Berry. Remember the earlier personal space comments? Just walk out into the audience and stand near the person who is typing. Don't look at him; just hover a bit, pretty soon the device will be put away. You never want to appear like the stern school-teacher, but you have to maintain control of your audience.

Direct eye contact allows you to have a one-on-one connection with each member of the audience if you are pitching to a group. If you keep direct eye contact with a person for a complete thought or sentence, then you have engaged that person and you have narrowed your audience to one for a few seconds. Be sure to move on to another person after that thought. Locking eyes with just one person throughout your whole pitch can make that listener uncomfortable and alienate the rest of the group.

Watch Out

Beware the distraction of the smiling, nodding, supportive listener. This person is being nice and trying to help you along by sending positive affirmations through body language. You will be tempted to home in on this one person and never look at anyone else. *Don't do it!* Chances are that person is *not* the decision maker. Also, you are neglecting the others. Their attention will soon wane because you are rejecting them for this one favored person.

Don't Let Them Get Away

While you are looking out into the group, take responsibility for what you are pitching. If the people in the room aren't listening to you, set your ego aside, forget about yourself, and focus on them.

> **SalesPEAK** Secret: You want to be proactive when you see any signs that a buyer is becoming preoccupied during your pitch.

Customers will give you signals if they begin to drift. Pay attention! You want to be proactive when you see any signs that a buyer is becoming preoccupied during your pitch. Take a look at the following Audience Messages and learn what each one means so that you can counteract it.

AUDIENCE MESSAGES

Arms crossed? Could be a negative, closed signal. But it could also mean that he's cold, that his chair has no arms, or the table is too high or low. Work especially hard to warm up to this person with eye contact and smiling. Note, though, that some attention-deficit or hyperactive people cross their arms to pay attention as holding them helps to keep focused.

Sleepy? After a high-fat lunch or one loaded with trypto-phans (the compound found in foods like turkey), people are often sleepy. So if you're making a pitch after lunch and see that people are slipping into an after-meal coma, shake things up; have people stand, come to the front to look at a demo, or even take a bathroom break if it's a particularly long presentation for a complex pitch.

Confused look? Check your use of jargon and special-ized words. You may be talking about your product or service, but not connecting with your audience because they do not understand your pitch. Stop and find another way to explain what you are talking about. Props help a lot at this point. They make you talk about your product in very concrete ways; most people identify with this—and it will help to regain their attention.

Drumming fingers or rocking? They may be impa-tient because you have gone on too long. People have short attention spans, as you may have noted. Check out the section on texturing your voice that follows; it will help you keep enough variety to maintain a lively pace that will hold everyone's interest. It could also be close to lunch, though. Check the time and use the shortened version of your pitch you've practiced.

Texturing Your Voice

Your conversational voice and your sales presentation voice vary from each other in volume, intensity, tempo, and inflection. You can use this sales-speak to your advantage to retain your buyers' attention. Make notes in your pre-sentation for building a crescendo, then back off suddenly and let your voice become measured and slow. Dramatic variations in speed and intensity will wake an audience up. Just be sure you don't hit people over the head with your points by yelling.

Put punch where appropriate—emphasizing certain words or syllables within words. Drag out important words— instead of delicious, say de-*lish*-us. Practice using your voice out loud to eliminate monotone. Remember that when you're uncomfortable, your vocal chords constrict and make you monotone. When delivering dull material, voice creativity is especially important. In a large room, the inflections (the natural ups and downs of the voice in speaking) become less noticeable because sound quality is lost.

In fact, any variation helps attention, especially a pause. If you've been speaking nonstop for over a minute, just stop for a few seconds. This unexpected interruption of the constant drone will let the audience catch up and will surprise them into giving you their attention.

Be Careful Not to Speed Away

The desire to recharge your buyers during your pitch might cause you to speed up. *Avoid that temptation!* Freight-train speech eventually falls into a predictable rhythm and becomes difficult for listeners to understand. By paying special attention to how you pronounce your words, you will slow down a bit, allowing the audience to get the meaning of everything you say. Focus on your pronunciation and you will eliminate the attention-killing fast talk.

SalesPEAK Secret: Focus on your pronunciation and you will eliminate the attention-killing fast talk.

Change the Channel

One of the most effective techniques for gaining and holding audience attention is to be sure you tune to the right "channel." We all have preferred pathways for taking in important information—sometimes even excluding others completely. Some prefer to read, some process better if they see ideas represented in a drawing or diagram, some become more engaged if they can move around while listening.

Below are several processing channels that you can expect to find among your buyers. Try to determine which channel you prefer. You likely deliver information on the same channel you prefer to use when you receive it.

PRINT: "I WANT TO READ IT."

Examples: Bullet points on a slide, handouts, outlined proposals, writing on a whiteboard, brochures

Strategy: Remember that if there is anything to read, the print person will read it over and over and not hear your speaking. Turn off the slide after everyone has seen it. Give out handouts at the end. Prepare "backbone" notes. (These are your main points with blanks that they can fill in from your material—seldom used in sales presentations, more effective for training.)

VISUAL: "SHOW ME A PICTURE OR DIAGRAM."

Examples: Schematics, flow charts, process diagrams, line drawings, photos, videos

Strategy: Think of visual or diagrammatic ways to get across what you are saying. If you aren't visual yourself, consult someone who is and tell that person you need a drawing or chart for an important point, ask them what they think would be a good visual representation of that point. Remember, bullet points on a slide are *not* visual; they are only print with color.

AUDIO: "TELL ME."

Examples: Speeches, recordings, testimonials from customers, music

Strategy: Be *very* careful with this channel. Many decision makers prefer that you "tell me the short version." However, listening alone is not an efficient way to gain and store information. Sixty percent of what we hear is lost in a week or less. If you have an advocate in the audience who will help you with pushing the sale, make sure that person really knows and understands your product so he can support what you have said after the presentation is over. Getting the members of the audience to repeat or discuss your ideas will also help win over audio processors.

INTERACTIVE: "CAN WE DISCUSS THIS?"

Examples: These are the buyers who process by speaking and carrying on a two-way exchange.

Strategy: Group discussions or sharing information with someone seated nearby are useful ways to pitch to this type of person. Questions and answers (questions asked by you) are a bit tricky because you don't want to surprise or embarrass anyone, though they can create exchanges. "Tell me . . . " questions that will pull impressions about your product or the need for your service from the audience members will engage those people who retain best from interactive pitches.

KINESTHETIC: "MOVING AND THINKING."

Examples: People who move around while they are on the phone or who like to take a walk when thinking through an important decision. These are also people who have difficulty sitting; they will rock in their chairs, swing legs, and so on.

Strategy: Bring audience members to the front for a role-play or do your presentation while the listeners walk around the facility. You could even set up a game of golf to pitch your products to your buyers. If you have a particularly hyper decision maker (or several), you can gain an advantage with this person by finding ways to give presentations while moving; you will rescue them from the confinement of an office or presentation room.

HAPTIC: "CAN I TOUCH IT?"

Examples: Product samples, interactive demos, props, manipulatives (a manipulative is something the audience member holds).

Strategy: If the customers put their hands on it, they are more likely to buy into it—idea or product. Also, haptic types pretty much only remember from your presentation the ideas that were connected with something concrete—a sample or some sort of promotional gadget that you relate to the product or service.

Since you have no control over what types of processors your buyers will be—and likely won't be able talk with everyone to learn their channel preference—you will have to texture your presentation to meet everyone's needs. You are probably starting to wonder, "How many different ways should I present my major ideas?"

The answer, of course, is "several." Limit the number of points you make and increase the number of different channels you use to make those points. Remember, you are going to be most inclined toward (and comfortable with) the style that is your natural channel. Professionals move past their own comfort zone to score with *all* the audience members, not just the ones who are channel compatible.

> **SalesPEAK Secret:** Since you have no control over what types of processors your buyers will be—and likely won't be able to talk with everyone to learn their channel preference— you will have to texture your presentation to meet everyone's needs.

Naked Scenarios

The two naked salespeople-in-training, Kyle and Lindsay, have prepared their presentations and taken their coaches' tips to heart. Now it's time to see them put everything into action.

Working Together for the Sale

Kyle's presentation skills coach called. "Kyle, it's time that you and Brian got together on how you're going to do your handoffs."

"What do you mean? He does his part and then I do mine."

"Actually, it's a little more involved than that. Remember, every word and every movement and every action that occurs during a sales presentation has to be strategic."

"Okay, I'm buying the whole strategy thing now, but what else do we need to do?" Kyle began to fidget with his pen while he held the phone in the other hand.

"Just have Brian come to Wednesday's session at 4:30. Planning is *everything*."

* * *

"Hello guys." Kyle's presentation coach greeted the two men as they entered the room. "Let's get down to business . . . you are presenting together to an audience that has multiple processing styles. You're both going to have to stay on top of your game. Decision-makers come in all shapes and sizes."

"Super! Let's get started! I'm ready to go!" Brian jumped up, strode quickly to the front of the room, turned to face Kyle and the coach. He smiled broadly and rubbed his hands together.

"No," the coach giggled. "When you smile and rub your hands together it suggests to the audience that you're planning something sinister. No touching of hands, no holding them across your abdomen, no rubbing them together."

Kyle laughed. "Yeah Brian, no hand-holding."

"The audience looks at your face but also follows your hands," explained the coach. "Let's work on creating visuals with your body."

As the pair divided up which parts of the new presentation Brian was going to do and which parts Kyle would handle, the coach worked with them on their body language.

"Now, Brian, you're the projected-sales-figures guy. The money guys will be really tuned in for this part and you're going to have to make them see dollar signs with your bikes."

Brian objected, "But the figures are right there! I've got the charts on slides and . . ."

Kyle put out his hand to stop the coach as she started to rebut, "This one's mine." He smiled as he got up. "They have to *really* buy into what we're saying, so we have to make them remember by using more than just a bunch of numbers." Kyle walked to the side of the screen and gestured to the numbers on it but took a small, toy bike out of his pocket as he did.

"It's hard to know exactly how much revenue to expect from any new product, but think of it this way." He moved away from the screen and pressed the "b" key to black out the slide. "Adult bikes sell well in the spring and fall because the weather's nice, right?" While he talked, he pushed the toy bike in an arc upward, back down, then upward again, miming two peaks. "But what if you had a cool bike by the same company to sell to the adults whose kids are getting out for summer and need something to do and then the same scenario to the fall buyers as Christmas is approaching?"

He started the toy bike low again and moved it up a smoother, but steadily climbing line this time. "You've helped even out that revenue rollercoaster by having two offerings from the one quality company."

Brian turned slightly toward Kyle, a surprised look on his face, then back toward the coach, who was equally impressed.

And It Begins

Knowing that the company's marketing professionals would be joining the IT professionals at this sales pitch, Lindsay took time to tweak her sales presentation.

She figured that the marketing people were most concerned about their webinars and receiving troubleshooting help any related software and hardware issues. Also, she assumed since they were in marketing that they would be visual processors, possibly looking for interactivity during the presentation. Having met with the IT manager pre-pitch, Lindsay knew that he was an audio processor—he was a "give me the short version, but it better be right" type of guy. She needed to create a presentation that appealed to both types of processors.

* * *

As people came down the hall toward the presentation room, Lindsay introduced herself.

"Hello, Ed how was your vacation?" She smiled, shaking hands. To another attendee she offered, "I'm so glad you've come. I know you're really busy and thanks for carving out the time to be here."

To the operations manager that she had spoken with previously, "I understand from our phone conversations that this is a really important part of your business and I'm really excited about the opportunity to present our solutions."

Lindsay strategized that with this type of firm the opening should be more illustrative and less flashy. Therefore, she opened with a brief recording of a helpdesk situation gone bad.

* * *

About halfway through her promised fifteen-minute sales presentation Lindsay shifted gears. She was losing the audience's attention with too many slides and someone had turned the lights down without asking. Instead of embarrassing this person, she decided to continue her presentation. To correct the situation, she walked around the room as she spoke, eventually ending up at the back of the room, giving her an excuse to turn the lights back on.

Gesturing with an open hand toward Brandon and Sheila from marketing, she asked a question to re-engage: "Sheila and Brandon, about how long do your training webinars last?"

Sheila answered, "We try to keep them to fifteen minutes with as long after as they want for questions."

Lindsay moved a few steps closer to them as she made her next point. "I've brought one of your helpdesk tickets here that says you lost a sale because not everyone could get onto the call and the screen at the same time."

Brandon chimed in, "That's right. It was my client, too."

Lindsay handed Brandon a stopwatch. "If you spend three minutes on each slide and you call in to our helpdesk as soon as you realize there is a problem . . ." She paused and gestured to Brandon to press the timer on the watch. ". . .Our helpdesk technician can pull up your webinar and the phone connection information and manually patch everyone in before you get to your next slide."

She made random eye contact around the room to hold the other decision makers' attentions, but then came back to Brandon. "Stop the watch now. If I'm correct, that was about twenty-five seconds. Our 'instant alarm' system codes will be given to each department, so that every time a revenue-feeding helpdesk issue comes up, the technician will respond in the twenty-five seconds that just passed on the watch."

Lindsay took back the stopwatch and directed her steps, slowly and methodically toward the IT personnel that were there. "But marketing isn't the only department that has rapid response needs, is it?" Several of those seated closest to her rolled their eyes. "Yeah, your group has to keep the entire system up and running with constant troubleshooting especially on the customer support end. What happens when your offshore contract help-desk support techs leave for the day? Something like this?"

Lindsay had gradually worked her way back to the table at the front of the room where there were papers stacked about two inches high. With everyone focused on her, she swept the papers off the table into a trashcan. "Your people are left thinking their tickets are being worked on, when in fact, they've been deleted." She placed special emphasis on the word *deleted* and picked up the trashcan to show around. "Sorry, you can wait all you want, but we're not calling you back. Right?"

She paused and made direct eye contact with each of the IT representatives in turn. "Now your managers are going to get a phone call because the ticket needs weren't addressed, and who's going to have to stop what you're doing and walk over to an angry employee to fix something that should have been a helpdesk item? Hmm?" She nodded toward Shelby, the software systems support tech. "Would that be you, Shelby?"

Shelby cringed and the others in her group nodded and murmured in sympathy.

Lindsay turned back toward her "home" spot at the front of the room and smiled a little smugly to herself at how well that had worked.

Momentum Management

The ways to keep the audience attentive and following you include:

- Moving eye contact around the room
- Stepping out into the audience
- Changing your voice speed, inflection, and intensity often
- Texturing your point delivery to reach all channels
- Using your body language and facial expressions
- Returning to you power stance regularly
- Pulling audience into points with movement and props
- Avoiding excessive use of "informational" slides

N-A-K-E-D sales presentations are all about *keeping* your buyer with you throughout the presentation. Spewing forth a monotonous and canned script in a nonresponsive and uninteresting way interests no one. You must remember to monitor the audience for signs of boredom or confusion so you can combat it as soon as possible. The best speakers can shift gears at a moment's notice in response to listeners' body language or verbal messages.

Chapter 5

HANDLING THE TOUGH QUESTIONS

SALES SITUATION: I'm afraid they'll attack me with their questions.

> Imagine yourself moving up and down the mat, thrusting your epee at your opponent as you attempt to protect your own hit zones. You came into the fencing match with a particular strategy and thought you knew your opponent, but now he's enacted an offense that has thrown you off your game. You need to know how to react quickly and alter your strategy in order to connect with the winning strike.

Sound a little like the question-and-answer session during your last pitch?

For a sales call Q&A session, you also have protection—maybe not a padded jacket, gloves, and a mask like in fencing, but certain strategies for parrying, blocking, and capitalizing on what comes at you from the buyers. As long as you are exchanging thrusts, you still have the chance to pull off a coup and win.

Selling naked creates a natural order for exchanges with the audience. You are able to organize and present just the right combination of information and persuasion *before* the decision makers can ask questions. The setup is all up to you. In this way you can defuse many concerns or questions in advance. The Q&A session is inevitable. But it will be the time to *really* put to rest any issues or objections your buyer might have that are acting as roadblocks between you and that purchase order.

So, welcome the time for questions. Be confident and sincere. Remember, if customers are talking, they are creating an opportunity for you to close the deal. The Q&A is their time to talk and the naked salesperson's chance to go for the winning blow.

E—Engage questioners in positive dialogue.

Go in Ready

In this chapter we will cover the necessary techniques that will help you to come across as brilliant and credible—two important attributes of a salesperson whom customers will be confident doing business with. Don't think for one minute that slick, skillful answers just occur "off the cuff." When you hear interviews with famous people, know that those people are coached and drilled on what to expect and how to answer certain questions. That's why they sound so good: they're not surprised! They went into the interview expecting the types of questions that were going to be asked, and they had an idea of how prepared speakers were going to answer them. They didn't even really have to think when delivering their answers on the spot.

Guess, what? You can be the same way. Your best protection is preparation. Just as a fencer has to learn defensive and offensive maneuvers *before* ever facing an opponent in a match, you need to get into your customers' heads and learn to expect their opposition. What are they likely to ask when you get to the Q&A session?

*Un*dress Rehearsal

The techniques in this guide are meant to turn you into a *naked salesperson*, someone who can be him- or herself and connect with others. When you truly connect with people, you can anticipate what they will ask. And if you can anticipate what your buyers are going to ask, you can develop good answers prior to your meeting so you don't have to do that whole squirming, fidgeting, deer-in-the-headlights routine. Instead, you can be excited to solve the problem, address the concern, or field an objection. You know the feeling. Someone poses a question to a group and you say to yourself, "I got this!" You can have that same feeling on a sales call. You just need to be prepared.

> **SalesPEAK** Secret: If you can anticipate what your buyers are going to ask, you can develop good answers prior to your meeting so you don't have to do that whole squirming, fidgeting, deer-in-the-headlights routine.

In order to anticipate the kinds of questions customers will be asking you, you need to undress why the buyer would be asking a follow-up question after listening to your presentation. Post-pitch questions usually fall within one of the following three categories:

General information: some detail the customer missed

True objections: implementation or financing concerns

Sniper shots: attempts to make you look bad

This is where your thinking ahead and writing important points down is *very* important. No surprises. Ask for help from others to think up possible questions. Go over your pitch with someone that you work with or are close to outside of work. Once you finish your presentation, see what types of questions they have for you. Try to address and make a mental note of the answers that you know (but took a little time to come up with). For matters of policy or pricing, be sure to consult official sources in your organization to ensure that you say only what is correct and lawful.

Everyone has heard the adage, "Never let 'em see you sweat." Well, don't let the audience see you *surprised* either. Second-guess your preview listeners; really make them think about what could come up as a potential question. The more thorough their review, the more prepared you will be. You will be able to handle calmly and deliberately any kind of question that comes your way. You always want to be prepared, as the Q&A could be the chance you need to complete the sale.

Here are some more specific directions on how to tackle each type of question.

Manage the Generals

Your rehearsal vetting should be enough to figure out what most of the general information questions will be. Since you already know your product inside out, answering those should be no sweat. If you're worried about being caught off guard by a question on some technical detail, bring one of the product technicians with you on the sales call, so you can consult his expertise during the pitch. Be wary of turning a hard-core engineer loose, though. Their level of detail may overload your business-minded buyers. Better to confer on a question, then answer it yourself.

> **SalesPEAK** Secret: If you're worried about being caught off guard by a question on some technical detail, bring one of the product technicians with you on the sales call so you can consult his expertise during the pitch.

Reverse the Objections

The true objections are easy because you should have received training in handling objections and how to counter them before you went out to make your pitch. *What?* You didn't? Then it's time for some homework. Round up marketing people (if your company has them) and other salespeople and take an hour to brainstorm objections everyone has heard about the product and any more you can dream up. Then, with the group there, discuss what a best answer would be. Take notes and go over them frequently so that responding to this type of resistance becomes natural—remember the idea here: so comfortable that you can do it *naked*.

Take Cover from the Sniper

Finally, you may get the heckler-type questions; these come from the type of person who does not have enough interest to make a constructive comment, but wants to ask a question in order to receive some much-needed attention. That's a group we'll call "shooters," and we will go over your strategy for dealing with them later in the chapter when we deal with the "live" Q&A session.

Start Up the Q&A

Now that you've had a chance to prepare for the Q&A session, it's time you learn how to work one into your pitch. Since you are in charge of the presentation, you continue to make that clear with a strong transition, like one of the following:

"And now, before I close, are there any questions?"
"Before we close this presentation, what questions do you have?"

Since questions can help you to direct the thinking of the decision makers, you may want to plant a question or two to get things started. Choose a "friend" in the audience, someone whose department stands to gain from the purchase of your product or service. Chat with her before your presentation and ask for help in getting the Q&A session rolling.

Once you've opened the floor up for questions, remember to stay cool—you've anticipated most of the questions they will be asking. But, they don't know that. Resist the urge to fidget, shift in your position, or avoid eye contact.

> **SalesPEAK Secret:** Once you've opened the floor up for questions, remember to stay cool—you've anticipated most of the questions they will be asking.

Remember, you *want* questions. An unvoiced question can kill a sale. You definitely don't want decision makers thinking of questions after you leave. So, encourage the dialogue; it is your opportunity to really shine.

And It Begins . . .

After you issued the invitation for questions, stand with your feet flat on the floor, approximately a shoulder's width apart, and with your arms relaxed at your sides. Pause and wait. Be sure that you have a pleasant and welcoming look on your face. (You might even want to practice this in advance.)

Step 1: Size Up the Questioner and the Situation

Who is this person? Why does he want this information? How can I best present it?

Your brain processes trillions of nerve impulses constantly; you have the opportunity in only a second to analyze and prepare at this high-speed thinking pace. This prepares you for step 3.

Step 2: Confirm the Question While Creating a Purpose Statement

For example: "James has asked me to comment on the amount of downtime you can expect for installation." Match the original wording as closely as possible to show that you were paying attention. Some very capable speakers write questions down. This helps them to focus. Our listening memory isn't always reliable.

If it's a question you had hoped for, thank the questioner.

"Thanks, James. I appreciate your giving me the opportunity to comment on this logistical question." This response lets the audience know that you will affirm people who ask legitimate questions, and it sets the tone for a positive Q&A time.

Step 3: Organize Your Response into a Three-Part Delivery

For example, "There are three main points I want to share with you regarding this installation that are going to make it go well."

Note: When you indicate that there are "three main points, ideas, thoughts, objectives, or challenges, avoid using the word "thing" as a noun.

Deliver your three parts like this:

"*First*, I have had our IT folks analyze your current system for possible interface issues. They have already built the patches necessary.

"*Second*, the installation will only take twenty-four hours, and that includes testing.

"*Finally*, this can be done over a holiday weekend when your system is pretty much shut down anyway."

Step 4: Put Closure to Your Response.

Your last step in the process is simple. Just repeat your purpose statement to close: "Now that you've heard about this implementation and how easily it updates, I recommend to all of you that you invest in this program to reduce your costs." (*Done.* Period.)

Answer sessions like this need to be *short*. The biggest challenge is to keep from talking *too* much! Avoid going back into a lengthy discussion from your presentation. If you go beyond a minute, you have spoken too long. Most people tune out after forty-five seconds. Dazzle 'em, then quit.

SalesPEAK Secret: Answer sessions like this need to be *short*. The biggest challenge is to keep from talking *too* much!

You should be prepared for most questions if you have done your advance work. But, if you are caught by surprise by a question, you still have to maintain a strategic approach. In other words, you cannot react immediately and blurt out whatever you're thinking or feeling at the time. By going through the Sell Naked steps above, you will take the time to formulate a quality response. As you have probably learned in your life, not all immediate responses make us look good.

> **NAKED TIP:** Whatever the type of question, you still follow the flow: engage with message-matching and management. Here's how that works:
>
> 1. Listen and process the question.
>
> 2. Repeat (mirror) the question for the audience.
>
> 3. Construct a three-point response.
>
> 4. Tie your response back to the purpose statement.

A Real-Life Example

An example of this occurred when JetBlue faced the "Valentine's Day Debacle" of 2007. It was icy out, and JetBlue kept passengers on a runway for nine hours. When CEO David Needleman was interviewed about the situation by a reporter from *Fast Company* magazine in the magazine's May 2007 issue, Mr. Needleman snapped:

> For the fifteenth time, we've learned from this. . . . I'm disappointed. Bitterly disappointed. . . . You're overdoing it. Delta screwed people for two days, . . . okay? So go ask Delta what they did about it. Why don't you grill them?

Ouch! What would a psychologist call that? Deflecting, maybe? Sounds more like he didn't follow any kind of strategy and ended up making his company look bad in the media. Keeping your temper in front of an audience (including the media) is essential to your success.

SalesPEAK Secret: Keeping your temper in front of an audience (including the media) is essential to your success.

Body Messages

In an audience situation, you have to recognize the effects of body messages as well as word messages. Other behaviors that can send the wrong signals include:

- Shuffling one foot or scratching your head—**submission**
- Touching your face—**nervousness or deceit**
- Clenching your fist (even at your side)—**feeling threatened**
- The Fig Leaf stance: hands crossed over your groin—**vulnerable, clueless**
- Hands in pockets—**insecure**
- Eyes moving back and forth, avoiding eye contact—**untrustworthy**

In addition, a river of perspiration running down your sides and darkening your shirt or blouse sends a negative signal to the audience. This is one reason most speakers keep a jacket on.

On the other hand, positive body language in response to questions is:

- Direct eye contact—**trustworthy**
- Relaxed muscles around the eyes—**enjoys talking with people**
- A momentary upward glance—**suggests thinking**
- Walking out into the group—**comfortable, nonthreatened**
- Chest raised, arms relaxed at sides—**"I've got this; I'm okay."**

Your audience is able to pick up on all your body's cues—negative and positive. Make sure your body language is communicating the right things.

NAKED **SALESPERSON STUDY:** Jason

During the question-and-answer portion of his presentation, Jason, a fairly accomplished speaker who was introducing a large IT initiative, was asked a question by a senior executive. "What's going to be the date of the rollout?"

Jason hesitated, removed his glasses, and rubbed his eye as he answered.

Perhaps his eye was burning or itching and he wanted to address that before answering. His nonverbal communication, however, suggested that he wasn't telling the truth. (Stalling, hiding his eyes, and choosing that particular moment to wipe a smudge off of his glasses—very telling.)

NAKED TIP: No one expects you to know everything. Have you noticed how some speakers will defer a question to an expert they have brought with them? Don't be afraid, especially in cases of technical presentations or sales proposals, to bring the product expert with you or the sales VP who has all the sales figures.

Remember, though, that you are the speaker; the audience didn't come to hear the accountant or the engineer. Consult these experts in advance with anticipated questions or have them handy to offer support, but be wary of letting any untrained speaker take your microphone position. This person may not have the training and expertise you do as a speaker.

Elephant Answers

This is a situation that speakers fear when they know that they are going to be put on the spot: What if I forget the answers that I have prepared?

The method below will ensure that you, like the elephant, will never forget.

Write your questions down in advance and practice answering them *aloud*.

> **SalesPEAK** Secret: Write your questions down in advance and practice answering them *aloud*.

Perhaps you may even want a colleague to role-play with. Just reciting the answers in your head will not help you to remember what you wanted to say. We're *all* good in our heads!

Do you remember taking tests in school? Tests that you had studied for days in preparation only to blank out when you were faced with the actual questions?

When we look at how the brain operates, we begin to understand why the old adage makes sense, "If you want to learn something really well, teach it." Setting up a memory storage and a memory bridge will make you relaxed and confident when questions come at you. To set up memory storage, you will want to:

1. Read or ask someone what a good answer might be.
2. Write down the answer (writing helps you remember).
3. Discuss the questions and answers aloud with someone.
4. Practice explaining the answer in response to a question.

Combining processing methods, such as hearing, sight, interaction, and so on confirms to your brain that you want specific information to go in and stay there until you need it—the answers to anticipated questions, for example. This is setting up the memory storage.

Practicing answers aloud in response to questions facilitates quick and smooth recall. Look at it this way, if you read a question that says, "What is four times four?" you can probably write the answer. But, if someone asks you aloud, "What is four times four," you may very well not be able to respond quickly and correctly unless you have given that answer in response to that question before.

The part of the brain that stores memory and the part that channels words out of your mouth are in two different places. A jump of a sort has to occur for an idea to get from the knowing part of your brain to the saying part.

Unless you create a bridge for those specific ideas that will answer questions, they will stay in storage when you try to speak them. Practicing answers aloud in response to questions will build a strong recall bridge, making it easy for you to get out what you really want to say.

Remember also that you may feel threatened if the speaker seems to be harassing you or trying to trip you up. Just treat each question as if it were nonloaded. In other words, use the same method you would for regular questions: confirm the question, give your three-part response, then conclude with a restatement of your purpose.

This accomplishes two things:

1. It keeps you calm and thinking clearly.
2. You display class and graciousness (which makes a heckler look bad).

Disarming the "Shooters"

Let's address the heckler, or what we call "shooters." If you understand what is behind their attacking behavior, you will be able to remain calm and in complete control of the situation. The expression "shooting off at the mouth" describes perfectly what is going on—the "shot" may not necessarily be aimed at you.

> **SalesPEAK Secret:** By making you uncomfortable, presentation saboteurs focus the spotlight in their direction.

The shooter doesn't intend to be confrontational. Shooters like to call attention to themselves. By making you uncomfortable, presentation saboteurs focus the spotlight in their direction. Some do this because they just like to stir things up; others may feel the need to mark territory in some way—to illustrate their expertise in the middle of your presentation. The toughest shooters are those who know you and know what your "hot buttons" are. These latter customers take a sniper's aim because they have a very specific target in mind.

NAKED SALESPERSON STUDY: Ann

For example, when she was under duress, Ann's neck would turn a deep shade of scarlet. One of her "shooter" colleagues, Tom, would draw unnecessary attention to her neck color whenever she had an important presentation. Once Ann learned that Tom was just going for attention, she was able to more calmly handle his "attacks." He ended up finding another target to harass.

Protestors

First, let's look at the protestors. Some of these folks are just bored and are trying to liven up the proceedings at your expense. For most, it's a power play. For example, a stirrer-upper will ask you something completely off the wall.

"Now, that's the new insurance plan, and we're asking each of you to choose the one that will suit your family situation the best. Before I close, any questions?"

"Yeah, I have one. Why do I have to pay the same for my two kids as Sam over there does for his six?"

Now, analyze what is going on here. Someone has questioned an element of the policy that you have no control over. Remember, this person just wants to stir something up, but if you play it straight, then you can defuse the situation and deflate the heckler.

SalesPEAK Secret: When an audience member wants to stir something up, you need to play it straight, then you can defuse the situation and deflate the heckler.

"That's certainly worth exploring. Our human resources director tells me that the company averages the total number of children of all employees and absorbs the difference for varying families. You will, I think, find the level of care and the reduced co-pays a real improvement over our previous plan."

You acknowledged the questioner, answered factually, did not "take the bait," and closed with a benefit of the program that you wanted to remind everyone of anyway.

Smarty Pants

The second type of heckler, the "smarty pants," will attempt to catch you on a point of fact. This is not someone you want to play with because this person really does know more than you do on this single point. Behavior like this, though, is usually from someone whose self-esteem revolves around being an expert—the "go-to" person in the organization. He feels threatened by you, the speaker. So an attack to crack your credibility and redirect everyone's attention is emotionally necessary.

NAKED SALESPERSON STUDY: Ken

"Well, Ken, it sounds like you have given this a lot of thought. What are your ideas on the subject?"

Then you take the microphone to Ken and put it right in front of him to speak. Or, in an informal situation, take one step closer to Ken, relax, and indicate with a wave of your hand that it's his turn.

After Ken states his ideas, invite others' comments on Ken's statement. All this will give you time to think up a really good answer. If you agree with Ken, then it's over and Ken has done your work for you. "Ken, that sounds like a plan."

Plus, you have let others know that unless they want a microphone stuck into their faces, they'd do well to stick with legitimate questions.

A couple of different methods can be used with this type.

1. Do *not* engage; you will only look foolish as this questioner undermines your knowledge with his own.
2. Turn the spotlight on him and crank up the heat. (This is an especially good technique at meetings

where someone is trying this kind of maneuver with the well-placed question.) To do this, ask the person's name (if you don't already know it). Say the name, then comment on his familiarity with the situation.

3. Ask him to answer his own question, then have others comment on that person's answer.

As long as you remain calm and do not act surprised or flustered, you will remain in control of the presentation—no matter what the Smarty Pants says or does.

Button Pushers

Button pushers require that you handle yourself more effectively than them. Any speaker, or any business person for that matter, should know what kinds of topics make you uncomfortable and why. This is an important principle of naked selling. Once you recognize your shaky areas, then you will be able to resist overreacting to a questioner's jab.

SalesPEAK Secret: Once you recognize your shaky areas, then you will be able to resist overreacting to a questioner's jab.

The strategy is based on your brain's makeup. You can't intellectualize and emote at the same time. One operation sort of cancels the other out. (This is why you should never argue when you're angry—you can't listen or think.)

When you feel yourself becoming upset by a questioner's remarks, you just disconnect the emotion by saying to yourself, "Hmmm, why am I getting so upset over this situation? Maybe I'm overreacting because of something else going on with me. This certainly isn't worth 'losing it' over. Wonder what she's looking for with that question?"

After you have disconnected any feelings of anger or fear, then, you play it like any nonthreatening question. Treat the question as if it were a genuine concern and not an attempt to get you flustered. (This can be really helpful with media or in job interviews.)

For Example . . .

"What makes you think that your service offerings are better than the company we're using now? I just don't see it myself."

For your response you should confirm the question, "I can see where this is an important issue to you, and our . . . (list the advantages again, idea A, idea B, and idea C) will indeed improve the results over your current provider."

Remember that if you have a combative audience member, do not reward bad behavior. For example, thanking someone who has just "shot" you will only encourage him to proceed with more negativity. So, avoid saying, "Thank you for asking that" if you don't mean it.

NAKED TIP: Don't ask for confirmation from a combative questioner, as it can open the door for further argument. With a badgering or "shooter" type question, it is important to provide "data."

Naked Scenarios

As you can tell by the content of this chapter, the question and answer session at the end of a sales presentation is very important, and can be where a sale is made—or lost. Kyle and Lindsay have both worked hard on overcoming their fears and following through with their presentations. A strong Q&A session will help them seal their deals.

Thinking on His Feet

"By this point you've seen the possibilities of both the CrossTrainer and the CrossTrick bike in expanding your offerings in the Boomer market. Before I wrap up the presentation, I invite your questions."

Kyle comes out from behind the stand and faces the audience. His hands are relaxed by his sides and his face shows a slight smile of welcome.

A hand goes up. Kyle extends his hand, palm up toward the questioner and moves closer to the side of the room where the questioner is, still being careful to position his body to face the other side of the room. He recognizes the questioner from his greeting as Everett, the operations and purchasing agent for an outdoor recreation chain in the New England area. Since this is an operations person, he's likely going to be concerned about managing inventory and the logistics of storage.

He looks to Kyle and starts, "Our demand varies seasonally so we may need to order forty bikes at one time, then later only two bikes per order. Can you accommodate that in your production? You seem like a pretty small operation."

In an instant Kyle processes: *The real question here seems to be supply capability. I'll start there.*

"Everett, that's a valid question. I'd like to address the production element on two levels to take away any concerns you might have there.

"The first level is design. Our fabrication process is very quick due to the engineering of the frame itself. We invested time in prototype development for manufacturing up front, so production is more streamlined.

"Secondly, though, we have regional OEMs lined up for contract manufacturing in times of high need. We are aware, of course, that demand peaks during Christmas and springtime, and ramp up for those anyway."

While Kyle is talking, he moves a few steps toward the other side of the room, and occasionally glances at other audience members, but always returns eye contact to the questioner.

"So, you won't have to worry about having to store a lot of out-of-season bikes. We have a rapid response system in place to get you what you want when you need it."

Kyle pauses as he glances at the audience as a group, then back at the questioner.

"Everett, does that answer the question for you?"

Kyle managed to address a possible objection in a way that made the entire group feel included in the answer. Because he prepared in advance, he was calm and genuinely welcomed the question. It gave him the opportunity to move the customers closer to the close.

Lindsay Leads Her Q&A

"Now that you've heard the advantages of our company's helpdesk solutions, I'm sure that you will have some questions. I see that we're running short on time . . . so before I close, what questions do you have regarding our services?"

Rob of the company's IT department stands up immediately. "One concern we have is whether your company will be able to learn our unique proprietary actuarial software. If you aren't able to master the programs, I don't see how you could possibly assist us in any kind of useful way."

Everyone in the audience turns first to the questioner then expectantly to Lindsay, who processes the question and develops a strategy in just a brief second's pause. *Hmmm. This is a combative statement, not a question. If I waver on this, he'll be on me like a shark. Though I'm really tempted to present him with a particular finger on my right hand, I know the three-part technique is more strategically effective.*

She takes one small step toward Rob and makes direct eye contact, but remains relaxed in her demeanor. She pauses briefly then responds, "Rob, it's understandable that you would have a concern about your proprietary software. I can assure you that our team of IT professionals will be thoroughly trained on your system prior to the launching of the helpdesk for your firm. If you like, we would be happy to provide you with our training development process to allow you to feel more comfortable with the choice of our company.

"As an example of our technical abilities, we have another client who has developed an in-house supply chain software process and that customer was also concerned. Because our IT professionals worked closely with the designer, the helpdesk has achieved a 98 percent approval rating within sixty days of helpdesk of its launch. The client is delighted with the results."

As Lindsay responds, she trains most of her eye contact on Rob. To keep the rest of the room involved, she looks around briefly, yet she returns to Rob at the end, but doesn't hold the contact long. She takes a step back, and readies to take another question. But Rob's not through.

"Yes, but supply chain software is not nearly as complicated as our actuarial programs here." He obviously prides himself on being the resident expert and feels that this position is in jeopardy, so he must challenge Lindsay.

Because of her meticulous planning that involved anticipating questions just like the one Rob has asked, Lindsay smiles confidently then addresses this new jab.

"Certainly you are correct in your observations about the level of complexity, but you will probably agree that when you have highly skilled, qualified IT experts, they can become proficient at learning any type of software in a short time."

Lindsay is following the age-old advice: Never argue with customers because they are always right—even when they're wrong. She has nothing to gain by arguing with him and getting into a verbal sparring match at the front of the room. Her purpose is to get the sale with skill and integrity. By demonstrating that control in her question-answering methods, she is showing the group her company's professionalism.

She nods toward Rob, showing that the discussion is through then turns and strides slowly back to the middle of the speaking area. Addressing everyone again, she asks, "What other questions does the group have today?"

Find the Good in the Bad

But, do you see how the question, even though it was sent as a jab, actually allowed you to restate the benefits of your service?

Ultimately, questions are opportunities to engage your audience members in a dialogue that lets you clarify or reiterate your important points. If you treat them as red flags thrown out to bait you, you'll end up like the bull in the arena that charges into the matador's sword.

> **SalesPEAK Secret:** Questions are opportunities to engage your audience members in a dialogue that lets you clarify or reiterate your important points.

Remember, N-A-K-E-D selling is about *engaging* your buyers, so keep answers short and simple. (Maybe even practice answering with a timer to ensure that you don't go on too long.) You will be less likely to dig a hole for yourself if the answers are succinct. Entering back into the content of your presentation is not an option at this point. Focus on following the steps outlined, and the answer to *your* final question, "Are you ready to buy," will be, "*Yes!*"

Chapter 6

GET THEM TO COMMIT

SALES SITUATION: Now that I've finished, I need a commitment.

> Picture yourself behind the computer, typing up an e-mail to this person that you met through an online dating site, who you have been chatting with f-o-r-e-v-e-r. However, it has not gone any further than a few suggestive e-mails. You have toyed with the idea of meeting up in person, but your online interest has never made the offer. Chances are it won't happen unless *you* ask to meet. You need to have the confidence to ask for a commitment.

Just as cute emoticons on a screen don't always lead to romantic attachments, nods in an audience, or smiles around a table do not necessarily ensure action by decision makers. Presentations in a business setting should generate a transaction: a purchase order or customer trial. The commitment is the part where the business is done; it's the "*do.*"

You have to build both the logic and the excitement in the customer's mind, then move agreement to action. In this part of the Selling Naked process you:

D—Drive the *do*!

Closing Time

One-on-one sales calls and group selling presentations have many similarities, but the differences help us define "closing time." When you're one-on-one with a customer—in person or on the phone—you close when you receive certain signals: a nod, a smile, a couple "yes" answers in a row.

But for presentations that are put together to sell to a group, the close occurs at a specific place, where timing is based more on the clock than on the nods. Your preplanning lays out an order of delivery:

- Your attention-getter
- Opening with a purpose statement
- Three customer-specific points (with support)
- Question and answer period

Then the close, generally within the last few minutes of the time you have allotted to you.

You can blow any chance of a commitment by not honoring the time constraint placed on your presentation. Decision makers, if they have allowed colleagues and direct reports time off their work responsibilities to hear your presentation, demand that you respect the gesture.

> **SalesPEAK Secret:** When you're one-on-one with a customer—in person or on the phone—you close when you receive certain signals: a nod, a smile, a couple of "yes" answers in a row.

When customers agree to assemble a group to hear your offering, and they allot *x* number of minutes, then that is the "price" they are willing to pay to possibly find a new solution. Don't ignore the value to the customer of that investment and go over time. This is true even when you are operating with a time cut—where the customer surprises you with less time than originally agreed upon. You adjust your presentation so you can still deliver a dynamite close.

In the close you're going for the big "Oh, yeah!" on the faces of the major players. Leading up to that, though, there are other positive nonverbal signals you can look for·

- Nodding and whispering "looks good" to each other
- Note taking
- Solid eye contact

But, if you are going over time, no matter how good your presentation is, you will likely see:

- Looking at watches, PDAs, or phones
- Shifting in seats, crossing and uncrossing arms or legs
- Off-topic discussions with each other
- Flat expressions and avoiding eye contact

Respecting customers' time will earn you points toward a final sale, partly because so few people do it. Self-absorbed presenters are so taken with their own voice and the captive audience that they go on, and on, and on. They seem to think that more of their golden words will buy them a contract.

The opposite is actually true. Adjusting your presentation so that the close is reached at the appropriate clock time is a necessity for selling naked. When you have a presentation appointment, you can build to a perfect climax for the commitment. You may not have the luxury of "feeling the close," as so many one-on-one salespeople swear by, but you do have the advantage of committed time in which to make your case for the buy.

> **SalesPEAK Secret:** Adjusting your presentation so that the close is reached at the appropriate clock time is a necessity for selling naked.

The Commitment Close

Remember that the sales presentation has one goal: *Get the business*. The test is not how flashy your presentation was; the test is if you secured the commitment.

In order to accomplish that, going into the close you will have to address some naked realities:

- You can assume that your audience has already forgotten some important points.
- Decision makers may not feel any sense of urgency to act.
- The final points you make are the ones customers will take with them to support their decision after they leave you.

You want the customer to feel as good about the decision tomorrow as he did when he agreed today. (No one likes the "morning after" second-guessing.)

SalesPEAK Secret: The test is not how flashy your presentation was; the test is if you secured the commitment.

What can work to help your deals stick is the "recency effect." Basically, decision makers remember the last points they heard in a presentation. In other words, even if they drifted in and out during your presentation, you can still support a decision commitment with a carefully crafted close.

NAKED TIP: Though the "recency effect" will help the key players remember the facts in your close, information is not motivation or commitment. Be sure that you've created excitement about what you are proposing during your presentation and *again* at the end. People buy (and buy into) what engages and excites them. Be sure to raise their interest and make them care.

Real-World Caution

Caution with this idea, though. Even a great close can never make up for a major blunder. Naked speaking recognizes the humanness of an audience's reactions, and humans rarely forgive an insult. Look at this example noted by Steven Levy's article in *Newsweek* (December 24, 2007). Levy relates an incident where Mark Zuckerberg, the founder of Facebook, ruined the positive reception he was fostering with a slip of the tongue.

Zuckerberg raised a few eyebrows . . . when he told an audience to hire young people with technical skills. Said Zuckerberg, "Young people are just smarter."

His explanation for blurting a statement that would have alienated anyone over twenty-five in his audience was, "I hadn't really planned [the speech] more than five minutes before I talked."

Avoid Self-Sabotage

Unless you thoroughly plan, prepare, and practice your entire presentation, you run the risk of sabotaging the close. Insulted and offended customers are not likely to commit to anything you offer, no matter how well everything else in your presentation went.

SalesPEAK Secret: Insulted and offended customers are not likely to commit to anything you offer, no matter how well everything else in your presentation went.

Getting the commitment is the reason for your presentation (and a pretty good part of keeping your job). For this reason, you don't want to leave the structure of it to your random memory. What if the plane you're on has to land on autopilot during a storm? There's a scary thought! Pilot your own presentation strategy so that you land safely at the gate.

If you make a habit of asking clearly and directly for what you want, you can do away with all the fluff and techno debris that gets in the way of the "yes."

Let's look at the steps to getting what you want as you end your presentation:

- Regain the key players' focus after Q&A.
- Summarize important agreement points.
- Ask for a specific action with a deadline.

Before you can act on any of these principles, though, you have to pull attention back to you after the Q&A session.

The Snap-Back

Here's a hard-and-fast rule: Always reserve time for *you* to close after the Q&A. Never leave the audience's final thoughts in the control of questioners. Snap back the customer's attention by transitioning (not jumping) out of Q&A. Since you have already told the group that you will close after the question-and-answer section (remember your intro to Q&A?), your transition is the signal.

SalesPEAK Secret: Always reserve time for *you* to close after the Q&A.

Here it is. After you have deftly answered the last question, glance at your watch or the clock on the wall and say, "Looks like we've used up all our time for questions," then move right into your close. If you have a persistent questioner that won't be put off, take the question, answer it quickly, then move on.

You could even say, "Thank you for showing so much interest in this great (product or idea or service). Those of you with other questions, I'm happy to stay after to answer any of them."

Regain the floor and the audience's attention focus with not only your words but also your moves:

1. Return to the front of the room.
2. Step in toward the group.
3. Adopt your speaker's stance.
4. Make direct eye contact with the decision makers.
5. Smile while you pause briefly.

Make sure that nothing in your demeanor or facial expression conveys, "I can't wait to get off this platform."

NAKED TIP: "Thank you for your time" is the lamest of closes. Decision makers will have heard interesting information and may even agree with your logic. But if you stop there, you likely won't get the deal. Break yourself of this verbal habit and go for the commitment!

Consider the commitment close the true success part of your presentation. Make it clear that everyone must listen. Use a powerful, energized tone, but be very deliberate and smooth in your delivery. Once you have regained your customers' attention, you will need to remind them why they want to buy.

> **SalesPEAK** Secret: Make it clear that everyone must listen. Use a powerful, energized tone, but be very deliberate and smooth in your delivery.

Hit 'Em Again

The main decision makers may have been distracted during your presentation (even if you did everything possible to keep their attention). Because of this, you must give a last pound to the nails in the base for their decision. This should be *brief!* Do not at this time rehash or bring up points that you may have left out.

Your summary lead-in to the final commitment statement is not the time to try to elaborate again on your points. Don't dilute the *do* by throwing new content in at the end. If the close is too long, someone will think you are open for more questions. These can redirect the audience's attention away from the commitment you are building. Besides, if you haven't made a positive impression by this point, you have little chance of making it now.

> **SalesPEAK Secret:** Your summary lead-in to the final commitment statement is not the time to try to elaborate again on your points.

If you were in full *naked salesperson* mode during your presentation, you took note of the statements your audience agreed with the most. Now is the time to cement acceptance—but keep it brief!

For example:

"You've seen the 40 percent return in just six months on your initial investment, the improvement in rate of product turnaround time. Is this the savings you've been banking on?"

Or

"You've recognized the savings in upgrade costs, the dramatic reduction in network downtime, as well as the improved profit margin on client services."

The reason we repeat the main agreement points in the close is not just to fill in for those who may have missed something. As every advertiser knows, repetition is the key to *internalization*. That's a great word for this process, too, because when your decision makers internalize an idea, they adopt it as their own. When it's their idea, they are willing to act on it. This is why as presenters we offer our ideas first in our purpose statement, next in our explanation, and finally in our close to drive the decision, or the *"do."*

SalesPEAK Secret: As every advertiser knows, repetition is the key to *internalization*.

By summarizing, we remind the audience why the decision is a good one and build confidence in a commitment by reducing risk. But you must take that a step further and state exactly what is to be done as a result of agreement.

Define the *Do*

Use your purpose statement to help you define your final objective. Your *objective* is the *action* the customer will take as a result of agreeing to what you have outlined and explained. Agreement is good, but don't stop there; go for the commitment. So, for you to get what *you* want, what do the customers have to do?

They will:

- Sign
- Authorize
- Support
- Commit
- Move forward
- Vote
- Order
- Buy

If you are asking for financial backing for an internal project or for your business, ask for it during your close. It might sound like this:

"Since our profit margin is narrowing due to excessive repair costs on old equipment, and our interest rates are rising, now you see why we need to move forward on this project to meet our objectives this year.

"We need your support on this initiative. When you are asked to vote, say yes."

> **SalesPEAK** Secret: Your *objective* is the *action* the customer will take as a result of agreeing to what you have outlined and explained.

Time for the Money

What separates naked salespeople from just average salespeople is this next and final step—sealing the commitment with a deadline. Don't let the customer's handshaking and smiles spark the happy dance in you. Without a time set on the action, you could be looking at a long and drawn-out deal. When deal duration drags out, the potential for a change of heart, or worse, a change of decision maker, can increase dramatically. In short, drag time can smash your carefully constructed money tower.

> **SalesPEAK** Secret: When deal duration drags out, the potential for a change of heart, or worse, a change of decision maker, can increase dramatically.

In going for the deadline, though, be effectual and not just impressive. When people sign their name on an important document, they often add a flourish at the end. Your flourish at the end of your close is the time seal:

"If we're going to roll this out for your company by spring, we need your purchase order by December 2nd."

"Because the holiday is coming up, you can have the software installed and tested before everyone is back on Monday. Just authorize the proposal by Friday the 18th."

You can even add a little extra punch by singling decision makers out, "Can I go ahead and get your commitment Barbara? Fred? Chang?"

The Answer—"Oh Yeah!"

Though everyone probably knows what the word "yes" sounds like, you should understand a few other ways customers send the "yes" message. They may:

- Nod and begin discussing implementation
- Say, "This sounds good"
- Invite you to lunch or to tour their facility
- Start discussing a timetable, "If we were to go with you, how quickly could you deliver?"
- Clarify numbers—with disbelief or excitement
- Stand up, smile, and give you an energetic handshake
- Introduce you to some others on the team (good sign)

Any of these signals would be cause for celebration. Get out your good pen for the contract signing.

Naked Scenarios

Now that Kyle and Lindsay have completed their presentations, they need to secure the buy.

Closing Time

Kyle and Brian were both exhausted. They had maintained a lively presentation that balanced business and technical concerns. Representatives for two large chains expressed definite interest throughout the pitch. Now it was time for the close.

Brian stepped up and nodded to Kyle.

"Thanks, man." Then he turned to the audience, adopted his relaxed but upright and solid speaker's stance.

"Today you've gotten a feel for how these two offerings from Crosswyse can help you ramp up your sales with both technical and business advantages." Brian clicked to a very minimal conclusion slide that outlined his main points, and continued speaking.

"The specialized geometry sets the seat back for easy walk-through and our patented sprocket gives full pedal power. As for our endorsements, Dar Jenkins is known around the world for his extreme biking and he enjoys making personal appearances at your stores. Also important for your customer service is our expert tech support—specialized technicians from our industry-leading program. Finally, you've seen how your margins will be substantial, due to our space-age aluminum alloy which yields ultra-light weight like the really big ticket bikes for a fraction of the production cost."

Brian paused and saw a few squirms from the tech-types. He headed them off with his close.

"I know that some of you will have more design questions for Kyle, since we have some pretty awesome innovations, and he'll be around all afternoon to chat with you. But now, can we go ahead and start looking at contracts and setting up some delivery timetables for you guys?"

Scal the Deal

As Lindsay worked through the end of her sales presentation with all the decision-makers in the room, she kept careful note of which benefits drew the most nods and body language agreement. As she moved into her close, those points received special emphasis.

"You've heard how our well-trained staff would handle your outsourced helpdesk, so I'd like to sum this up with the three main differentiators:"

She held up her hands and counted on her fingers with a brief pause after each for added effect.

1. "We can accommodate both your domestic and international offices
2. With our fifteen years of experience you can be assured that every helpdesk ticket is addressed and resolved
3. Our experts can be trained to accommodate your questions and your proprietary software"

Lindsay looked around the room as she closed.

"Now that you are clear about the advantages of our business, what do see as our next step? Could we go ahead and sign a contract?"

Angela, the head of purchasing, responded, "We're going to see one more presentation and then get together at the end of the month to decide this."

Lindsay maintained a positive and expectant demeanor by direct eye contact and a pleasant smile.

"Great! Is there anything else you need prior to that meeting?"

As she expected, Rob had to have his say, "Actually, we would like to see some documentation of your training success. In addition, it'd be nice to see stats like how many hangups, satisfied tickets, and lost calls your company has had.

Lindsay stifled a smug smile since she was thoroughly prepared for Rob's request. "I can get that to you by 4 P.M. today and can follow up on the end of the week. Should I call you or Angela?"

After she confirmed the follow-up with Angela, Lindsay shook the hands of everyone as they left, right on time.

The Naked *Do*

Remember that the most important portion of your N-A-K-E-D presentation is your driving the *do*, your close on a commitment, a specific *do* statement. If you leave and the decision makers say, "Jan really gave a dynamite presentation," that really doesn't mean anything without an action. Asking for the sale confirmation at the end of your presentation is not just one way—it's the *only* way to get what you want. After all, you're there to secure a deal.

SalesPEAK Secret: Asking for the sale confirmation at the end of your presentation is not just one way—it's the *only* way to get what you want.

Make sure you:

- Practice your close numerous times before you present
- State clearly what you want
- Close strongly with a deadline on your plan

Then, and only then, will you truly get what you want!

Chapter 7

TAKING YOUR PITCH ABROAD

SALES SITUATION: I'm an effective salesperson, but when I present to international customers, I feel like they just don't get me at all.

You are all set to jump in and play for the big bucks. You have been practicing and playing poker now for years. You can anticipate your fellow players' moves and bets each time a card is flipped, and place your bets accordingly. You're invited to play a game of cards one day and expect to take the pot. You've been doing this for a while now and understand how to play the game. Then you show up.

It's true, you were invited to play cards—but the game they're playing ends up being bridge, not poker.

It's a game of cards, yes, but the language, scoring, and dealing are very different. Selling in an international environment is much the same. The game is business, but the players adhere to different rules, and wins are scored by a different system on each side.

By this point you have become accustomed to the whole selling naked experience in American industry environments. You have shoved away the barriers between you and your audience and stripped off the layers that you were hiding behind. In short, you have embraced the naked approach to selling.

But the nature of naked is different to different cultures—especially in selling applications.

Let's look at how the salesperson adapts the naked selling process in a multicultural setting.

N—Navigate the system by building a plan.

Navigate the New Terrain

International sales are often multistep deals where you tiptoe through many levels of relationship building and business. Every presentation you give must play a carefully thought out part in that process. You will have to learn to be naked in many languages and many cultures.

> **SalesPEAK** Secret: Every presentation you give must play a carefully thought out part in that process.

For example, what are you selling exactly? The answer may depend on your client's culture as much as her need for your solution. Suppose you are doing a presentation on your company's ability to always meet manufacturing quotas for time and quality. Perhaps after Asian investors have looked over your company's technology and patents, you could be called upon to persuade them of the harmony and effectiveness of the management team.

The Japanese, for instance, are not going to spend a great deal of money on anything if they are not convinced that it is being produced by a strong and cohesive team. For this reason, your sales presentation will include examples of how well your group works together to solve problems while maintaining high standards. By the way, this presentation may be requested at the end of a congenial dinner over drinks—no slides, no notes, no handouts—naked!

Your presentation may appear impromptu, but if you have assessed your customers correctly and studied their buying behavior, you will be prepared with a masterful sales presentation. When they buy your people's competence and loyalty, you have made a sale. And, no matter how many "yeses" you may have received with your prior attempts to close, you are not done until they are sold on your company as well as your products. For this and many other reasons described below, selling naked to an international group is different and requires additional knowledge and preparation.

SalesPEAK Secret: If you have assessed your customers correctly and studied their buying behavior, you will be prepared with a masterful sales presentation.

Always Be Prepared

Planning and preparing should also include your learning, at the very least, a greeting in the native language of the country you are in. For example, taking extra care with Chinese and other inflected languages is critical because one word can have many different meanings, depending on the emphasis or pitch with which you say it. You wouldn't want to thank someone for the wonderful donkey when you meant to say hospitality! A lack of attention to a courtesy detail could blow your sale.

SalesPEAK Secret: A lack of attention to a courtesy detail could blow your sale.

Other parts of your planning activity should include a thorough study of the culture that you will be presenting within—particularly that culture's approach to business. Americans tend to think that everyone looks for the same benefits and the same "it's newer, shinier and better" generalities. Some cultures value traditions, especially their own. You will have to prepare your presentation to include ways your products or services support clients' existing products or structures.

Valuable Resources

There are a few "encyclopedias" of selling to international customers, but probably the best one is *Kiss, Bow or Shake Hands* by Terri Morrison and Wayne Conaway. This book not only gives you some helpful history on sixty different countries and their customs in a concise way, it also points out exactly where Americans are likely to stub their toes in communication and social/business protocols. And remember the first rule of planning a sales presentation to people from another culture: Don't assume you really know anything about them. It's not going to be enough to say, "Oh, I get the Latin guys. My friend Jay is from Colombia, so I'm already cool with those South Americans."

Really? Do you know that in Brazil they don't speak Spanish at all, but Portuguese? See? It's not as easy as it looks. For example: They are very sensitive and touchy, including greeting with an embrace and a kiss on the cheek. Eye contact will be intense, so you should be especially focused on that as you present.

SalesPEAK Secret: Plan your sales presentation with at least a basic knowledge of the people to whom you will be speaking.

Plan your sales presentation with at least a basic knowledge of the people to whom you will be speaking. There is a lot of money in international sales, but no matter how good you are at closing business on home soil, be prepared to put in a lot of hours of study to become as effective with customers of a different culture.

As you move to the next step in becoming a truly naked salesperson:

A—Approach the topic and the audience
with enthusiasm.

Approach Your New Buyers

As you are getting your sales pitch together and are ready-ing to interact with your buyers, you should take a moment and think about their cultural background. Some of the things you would do or say with American buyers would be seen as a faux pas if done or said to an international buyer. Here are some things to consider depending on where you are going to give the sales pitch.

Keep Your Enthusiasm in Check

Consider how that enthusiasm should be expressed. In some countries, more controlled enthusiasm is critical to your success. For example, with German decision makers too much of the over-the-top effusiveness is off-putting.

With certain cultures, lively body language including hand waving and animated expressions would be expected to show that you believe in your product and its ability to enhance the customer's business. If you are a more reserved type person, you might have to summon up the sales speak-er's persona to get the job done.

An excellent time to generate enthusiasm and confidence is during your welcome and greeting to the customers as they enter the conference room. The enthusiastic double-hand, vigorous, pumping handshake many Americans seem to favor would be quite a shock to a Korean, who doesn't believe in being touched by strangers. An Egyptian might take your outstretched hand, grab it, then hug you strongly.

Find a Common Ground

If you are dealing with Latinos, you will greet them with lively talk about family, not immediate references to the business at hand. Relationships are more important than business in many cultures and are the basis for customer relations. Conversely, politics is an accepted topic with the French, but any discussion of family is considered too personal.

SalesPEAK Secret: An excellent time to generate enthusiasm and confidence is during your welcome and greeting to the customers as they enter the conference room.

In fact, socializing may be part of your presentation; if you are introducing your product after a dinner, you should plan to spend the whole evening. In some cultures dinner is served eventually as part of an evening of socializing—not on any special timetable. So there is "always time for business later." You can be enthusiastic, but social protocols may take over. Understand this *before* conducting your sales activity.

Punctuality Does Matter

In Germany, as in the Netherlands, it's critically important to begin on time. The Germans value precision and punctuality and do not handle surprises well. For them, the socializing time and presentation time should be separate and mapped out in an agenda.

For the Women

Just a note for women in particular: Not only your greeting but also your ability to understand the role of women in the culture may determine the initial impression you give. Though many countries of the world follow Western dress protocols for negotiations and formal business gatherings, skirts for women are preferred for the best impressions. When presenting in Muslim countries, be aware of specific dress codes appropriate for women. In fact, you may find that in some countries women doing business in general may be frowned upon or may require an adjustment to specialized cultural dress.

Brief Your Team

If you are presenting with a team of people, ensure that everyone on your team is aware of these protocols in advance. Think of how a president or head of state prepares for an international visit with other heads of state. He or she is briefed in advance so that local customs are not violated inadvertently. It's the same for your sales presentation.

In the United States, obviously some of these ideas may be a bit overboard. However, people are who they are, and although most of us adjust to the place where we live, it's still important to consider who the audience is. To deliver to senior-level executives at a German company here in the states would require conservative clothes, proper handout materials, and a level of formality not necessarily expected in American companies.

Sometimes bowing, hugging, kissing both cheeks, or submissive behavior in greeting would make the best impression. Again, preparation for success is the key.

SalesPEAK Secret: If you are presenting with a team of people, ensure that everyone on your team is aware of these protocols in advance.

Adapt Your Pitch Style

And finally, your delivery must take different forms across cultures. Puffery or saying that your product is the "best" is considered dishonest and would be received badly in many places. An example is how the British carefully avoid overstatement about anything, products included. You would be expected to follow their lead in your own display of enthusiasm. To an even greater extent, Chinese customers will prefer a more matter-of-fact sales presentation—devoid of gestures and facial animation. In the same way, holding the attention of the audience throughout your sales presentation has its challenges.

K—Keep the audience with you throughout
your presentation.

Keep It Together

Often we like to read an audience while we are giving our sales presentation. We look for a nod or a smile, maybe even a certain eye contact that indicates interest. Some customers, however, are less obliging with supportive smiles or body language that shows great interest or acceptance depending on their cultural background. In part, it is simply that they see business dealings as serious and formal, but another reason is that a selling situation is a lengthy process and they don't want "tip their hand" in case of later negotiations.

> **SalesPEAK Secret:** Some customers are less obliging with supportive smiles or body language that shows great interest or acceptance depending on their cultural background.

One recommendation we have made in this book is that you use your personal power of physical presence to sell while presenting. Earlier we suggested that you walk out closer to the decision makers, even standing next to some customers while you are speaking. But keep in mind that this practice could be problematic, depending on what country you are in. An Asian person might feel invaded if you stand too close in a situation like a sales presentation. Cultures requiring a great deal of formality and protocol in business dealings might consider your leaving the front of the speaking area as unprofessional or too familiar.

> **SalesPEAK Secret:** Cultures requiring a great deal of formality and protocol in business dealings might consider your leaving the front of the speaking area as unprofessional or too familiar.

On the other hand, in Latin America and many other cultures, getting closer is a compliment and is necessary to truly persuade your customers. You may find, too, that many people from various countries have a different sense of space than you. Americans tend to keep approximately three feet from each other in conversation (or "arm's length" apart).

SalesPEAK Secret: If you talk too fast, it will make you sound arrogant and like a know-it-all.

The language barrier is a concern as well. If your customers do not speak English easily, you should revamp your presentation to a level similar to third-grade English and *slow down*. Your listeners have to process and translate in their heads while you speak. Also, if you talk too fast, it will make you sound arrogant and know-it-all. Avoid using abbreviations, such as HR, ROI, and such, which may not translate well. And remember also to avoid calling on a particular customer for a comment; that person may be embarrassed if his or her English is not so good.

E—Engage questioners with message matching and management.

Engage Across Various Borders

Q&A can require you to be on your toes even under the best of selling situations. But working with other cultures can challenge you further because questioning styles and purpose vary greatly. Where Germans may be very blunt and expect the same from you, Russians and Israelis take great delight in arguments—loud and full of hand-waving and gesturing—so be prepared for what seems like violent opposition in the Q&A part. In some other cultures, you will find extreme politeness and a noncombative approach during Q&A, or even a reluctance to ask questions at all.

But the greatest hurdle in Q&A comes with the use of interpreters. There is a wonderful set of guidelines for the use of interpreters in business exchanges in Brooks Peterson's book, *Cultural Intelligence*. His recommendation for questions is especially helpful. He suggests that since interpreters speak the language but are not *you*, you should always look at the questioner while the interpreter translates. In this way, you can observe the tone and body language of the customer while he or she is asking the question. Peterson adds that it is particularly important to stress to your interpreter that he or she should not alter the content or intensity of your words in any way. (This should be done in advance as part of your preparation.) You want to ensure that your exact meaning comes across, not a filtered or watered-down version.

An interpreter only translates your actual words; it is still your responsibility to adjust answers to the communication style of the culture you are addressing. For example, Chinese people, among several other cultural groups, appreciate a pause between the question and the answer. This shows them that the person answering respects their ideas enough to think about them before responding.

Another cultural quirk to watch for in Q&A is that the decision maker or the ranking person in the room will not ask a question. You might be able to pick out the power person by noting who asks questions and who does not.

You'll want to be careful using analogies when answering questions. American salespeople, males in particular, use quite a bit of sports language: "get to first base," "score a touchdown," "put into the penalty box." These comparisons are well received in the United States, but they are very much resented by customers in other countries where the referenced sport is relatively unknown. Analogies are excellent tools to help clarify the answer to a question, but avoid those related to American sports.

Whichever country you have targeted for your sales presentation, be sure to prepare for the following protocols in your Q&A section:

1. Know whether factual evidence or more personal or spiritual elements drive the decision so that you can support your answers correctly.

2. Anticipate the types of questions you will receive, and practice answering them in advance of the sales presentation.

3. Find out how eye contact is viewed—in some countries it is an absolute necessity or you will be perceived as lying, whereas in others a riveted gaze is considered disrespectful.

4. Never make a joke out of a question; few cultures view humor in business well, outside of the United States.

5. Understand to what degree "badgering" or disagreeing with someone in business is the norm. Sometimes this approach provides you with the respect needed to close the deal.

6. When using an interpreter, be certain to expect a longer time for translations of your exchanges, and practice standing there patiently with the right facial expression as the interpreter translates.

7. Be careful with absolutes, such as "no" or "yes" or "best." "No" is often considered impolite, "yes" has many different meanings, and "best" may have to be proven with mountains of data.

> **D**—Drive the *do* and gain commitment
> for your ideas.

Drive the Sale Home

Before you can close the sale with a powerful, persuasive ending, you must first determine your goals. Keeping in mind that various cultures communicate differently, you'll need to practice and prepare your close to have it down, cold. Fumbling, opening yourself up to a vague, ambiguous ending, or coming on too strong can kill your close. Remember, the purpose is to drive the *"do"* by moving the sale forward. Understanding and appealing to the specific cultural group you are presenting to will help you secure the agreement.

> **SalesPEAK Secret:** Keeping in mind that various cultures communicate differently, you'll need to practice and prepare your close to have it down, cold.

And since all presentations must eventually culminate in either a closed sale or a next step in the process, your understanding of the decision maker's culture, a well-crafted plan, and a powerful delivery are essential to your sales success.

We've talked in earlier chapters about reading body language and close signals, but the rules of that game vary greatly by culture. Nodding may be merely a supportive gesture to make you feel comfortable and honored. A hard, unyielding gaze, on the other hand, could mean serious concentration, rather than resistance or dissent. So we come back to learning cultural differences—not only the rules of respect but also the rules of conflict.

It is not at all uncommon for Russians and other Eastern Europeans to argue with you when they are showing respect for your ideas. Thus, resistance is really acceptance. In fact, one way to respond to this resistance is agreement, "Perhaps you are right. So you think that maybe it will not work for you?" You may see a complete turnaround at that point, with the customers beginning to try to convince you that your product will work!

One world-traveling colleague shared an experience. "I was working on a deal with a Chinese company and had met with the lower-level people over and over but never the decision maker. I had lots of assurances that they were very interested, but no one was signing anything. Then, unexpectedly at one of the meetings, a senior level guy came in and offered to show me his company's financial report. Apparently, that was the "buy sign," and we moved quickly after that on the details of the sale.

Earlier in this section you saw that doing business in international markets or with individual buyers from other cultures had different rules for what had to happen at what stages. Now is the time to apply this insight to defining the close. In high-protocol cultures you never get to step D without going through A, B, and C first. So you close on different outcomes, generally four or five, before any final signing. You must recognize also the meaning of time as it relates to a close. Americans love to be able to fly somewhere and "wrap up a deal" in a few days, then fly home.

Rushing is the best way to miss the sale, so each presentation you do should lead to a close that is appropriate for the way the culture does business. Granted, foreign-born customers living in the United States learn many of the ways of American business. But an Indian businessperson living in Corpus Christi, Texas, is still entrenched in Indian culture, *especially* when important decisions are going down. Knowing what represents a close at what stages will help you keep your presentations upbeat and focused and subdue possible frustration over not receiving a commitment after two, maybe even three, meetings.

SalesPEAK Secret: Rushing is the best way to miss the sale.

Naked Scenarios

While our naked salepeople showed they could land deals with other Americans, international sales are a whole other ballgame. Let's see how they perform when they have language and cultural obstacles to overcome.

A Bicycle Built for You

After a successful sales presentation, Kyle and Brian took their show on the road. Brian was contacted by a Brazilian hotel chain about the possibility of producing a customized model of the Crosswyse for its various resorts. Kyle—as always—was reluctant.

"Tell me why it is we're going to Brazil?"

"Because I'm a sales genius and have put together a very solid deal with two resort chains there to buy our bikes for their guests and their kids to rent. It seems that people like to ride bikes when they go there and the resorts want models made just for them. You know, like Crowne Plaza is doing with their beds." Brian explained trying to get comfortable in the airplane seat.

"So, we're going to have to design a whole new bike for these guys?" Kyle looked sideways at his partner, wondering if he'd lost it completely.

"No. We take the basic model, add something that looks, well, Brazilian, and paint them the resort's colors. And *ta-da*! A customized product."

"And why on earth would we want to do that?"

"Because the markup is huge for the customization process and they want 350 bikes the first year. Think you can handle that?"

"Yeah, I think we can handle that." Kyle chuckled. "We can definitely handle that."

In a few minutes Kyle nudged Brian again. "But Brian, I don't know any Spanish for the greeting."

"That's okay." Brian mumbled. "They speak Portuguese there."

* * *

"Okay, Kyle, do that engineering thing you do." Brian whispered as an aside to Kyle. And to the group, he said, "And now that you've learned about the revenue potential of bike rentals and sales for your resorts, our design engineer, Kyle, will share with you the special Resort Edition bike."

Kyle passed around some concept drawings. Since the customers all spoke excellent English, he was able to move among the audience members as they clustered around each set of drawings. He listened carefully to their comments and even made a note or two on the tiny spiral-bound note pad he kept with him. After answering a question or two about the different models, he stepped back to the front of the room.

"Families come to your resorts to enjoy spending time together. They want to leave the video games and television behind and see your beautiful countryside. To show you how this would be, I have a short video of Bibiana and Gervasia biking with their sons Luis and Marcos. Bibiana works at one of your resorts on the coast." Kyle darkened the room for the clip, but brought the lights back up immediately when it finished. "We will call your specialized design the *Cruzeiro da Estrada*. The bikes will have each resort's name and crest on them. Additional technical features include the use of tires made from your local rubber production facilities. We wish for our bikes to help preserve and add to your local economy . . ."

As the presentation closed, Kyle and Brian directed the hotel representatives to the resort dining room for a lunch hosted by Crosswyse Innovations.

* * *

"You really grabbed them with that family stuff. It's a huge value here, but most companies only market to singles. Most of our customers' guests are families. And the local resources thing? That was brilliant! Where did you get that stuff?" Brian congratulated Kyle.

"Engineers can read more than CAD drawings." Kyle responded with a confident, worldly grin.

To the Point

"Rachel, I really don't think I can do this presentation. How am I supposed to get through to people from *Germany?* I've never left the United States! Please cover for me?" Lindsay desperately tried to plead her way out of the afternoon's presentation.

"No whining. Besides, you of all people should be able to get into their heads. They're into precision and the numbers. That's *you!* You're all about 'getting it right.'" Rachel chided her.

Lindsay grumbled a bit. "Yeah . . . I guess . . ."

Rachel continued, "They see a flashy saleswoman like me and immediately they tune me out. But you have a very low-key, matter-of-fact approach to selling, and they'll go for it."

"Okay, okay . . . but how I am supposed to start my presentation?"

"Open with a greeting in their language. Remember, German is a very crisp and sharp language, so every sound should be clear. It's '*Guten tag. Wie gehts mit Ihnen heute abend?*'"

"But won't they think that I can speak German and start talking to me?" Lindsay continued to worry.

"Not with your pronunciation!" Rachel laughed. "But they'll be flattered you tried."

* * *

Lindsay arrived an hour before the presentation and set up the network computer and the phone-lines for the demo then went out for a break. When she returned fifteen minutes before the set time, three men and one woman, all in dark suits, were chatting and one other was messing with the computer. Lindsay greeted each, shook hands and gestured for them to take their seats.

She breathed in one deep gulp of air and began.

Though the looks were piercing in their scrutiny, Lindsay stood her ground during the technical questions. ". . .and you'll see from the test data from other American companies that shows our reduced wait and turnaround times."

"But what about your ability to handle international helpdesk calls?" One of the gentlemen asked.

Lindsay had some very quick thinking to do. She had been led to believe that her company was bidding only on the tech support for the American part of the organization; that she was just presenting to the German upper management because they liked to be hands-on with their divisions.

Her thoughts raced. *What is this? Is he just jerking me around or is he giving me an opening to talk about their European business as well? Better play this one really cool.*

"Thanks for giving me the chance to discuss our international set-up." She composed herself. "Our client in Berne had similar concerns because of the multilingual culture that Switzerland has. What we ended up doing was combining some local contract people with our . . ."

As she finally re-directed the sales presentation back to the close, Lindsay moved forward, "I see our time is up. I understand that you are very busy and have many demands on your time. So let's discuss our next steps together."

Connect with Everyone— No Matter Where You Are

One hard-and-fast rule of closing in cross-cultural selling situations: Be certain that everyone in the room (even if there are twelve to fifteen people) understands your product and its fit with the company's needs. It may not be immediately clear who the emissary of the decision maker is at first, but that person is your right hand (and mouthpiece) to the final sale with the higher-up. And any disrespect shown the emissary would be perceived as disrespect shown to the company.

> **SalesPEAK** Secret: Be certain that everyone in the room (even if there are twelve to fifteen people) understands your product and its fit with the company's needs.

Finally, enterprise is heading in the direction of foreign markets and sales to large, non-American accounts. There is business to be earned out there. Don't forget that those countries are buying from someone; it might as well be you. Learning an entirely new culture is time consuming and often difficult—especially learning the more subtle nuances of not only deal-making but of interpersonal relations as well. But with preparation and a genuine desire to understand the ways of your customers, you can zoom past the competition and secure the business for your company, which will, of course, reward you handsomely with a trip to a foreign country!

Chapter 8

PERFECT THE FOLLOW-THROUGH

SALES SITUATION: What about when I really need the extras to support my points? How do I know what to use?

Way back when, a successful salesman was a guy with a wagon who went town-to-town carrying his products and selling. Sometimes he would pull people in to purchase his wares by providing some sort of entertainment. Maybe there were a few magic tricks or some juggling, and if he was quite successful, he might even have a carnival-type act put on a performance to attract prospective buyers.

The idea was to draw customers, then sell them something. Today, we work by appointments, and the "magic" will take place during your presentation through effective delivery skills. Though we're considerably more high-tech now, the customer still needs to be engaged in the presentation. For a web-based "show," for example, you might not be using dancers or musical accompaniment but other attention-getters that will help you draw in the customers.

> **SalesPEAK Secret:** Naked selling is the purest form of connection with buyers, and every good salesperson knows when and what to add to ensure the close.

Throughout this book you have learned about various strategies to invite and hold customers' focus. Naked selling is the purest form of connection with buyers, and every good salesperson knows when and what to add to ensure the close. Strategic use of support tools can enhance what you are doing as long as you remember to stay as naked as possible.

These naked supporters are:

- Storytelling
- Segues
- WebX
- Teleconferences
- Humor
- Videos
- Flip charts
- Posters
- Whiteboards

The Naked Story

Sports figures, politicians, and various other famous people often speak as a second career after they are no longer national figures. You and I go to hear them if we are interested in their lives—we want to hear their stories. But we want to hear a well-told story, not just an hour of random, seemingly unrelated events strung together. Memorable salespeople not only have good stories to tell, but they also know how to work those stories effectively to make their sales.

Good stories are like any good accessory—tie, necklace, or belt; they enhance the presentation. So meaningful stories have a few elements in common:

They Don't Have to Be the "Truth, the Whole Truth, and Nothing but the Truth"

A speaker's story is a dramatized telling of an incident or series of events with the purpose of imparting insight or understanding and making a point. It does not have to have actually happened to you or to anyone around you to be a useful support. People have always enjoyed tall tales (Paul Bunyan, Grimm's tales, etc.), and even today tabloid newspaper sales attest to our continued interest in a good story, true or not.

Composites of stories, local-color stories with the names of the cities altered, combined incidents from several months compiled into one day—all these are stretches of the truth, but are illustrative of a point. Think of them as examples of how an event can play out.

Stories that ask "What if" are especially effective in sales situations. If you can effectively paint a picture in the mind of the customer of how great the future of the company can be with your product, then you likely can count on a sale. This is not a provable truth, but it is one possible outcome.

> **SalesPEAK Secret:** If you can effectively paint a picture in the mind of the customer of how great the future of the company can be with your product, then you likely can count on a sale.

Remember, though, trumped-up testimonials or test results are just lies, not stories with a purpose. Be sure that you understand the difference and plan your sales stories accordingly.

A Joke Is Not a Story

As noted earlier, you need to be very sparing with jokes because they are indeed only as good as the teller and most of us are not great joke tellers. In addition, what is funny to one group is not necessarily going to be funny to another. And the dead silence following a bad joke screams, "no sale here."

And any jokes the customers have heard before suggest that you have no originality and that the rest of the presentation will likely be awful as well. Not to mention that there is always the chance of offending someone with a joke. (A bit more on humor as a tool later.)

> **SalesPEAK Secret:** Using jokes the customers have heard before suggests that you have no originality and that the rest of the presentation will likely be awful as well.

Focus on the Physical

Practice your expressions, hand gestures, walking and talking, pronunciation (examples include: final endings, such as: "seeing" and "going" not "seein'" and "goin'" or "gonna"). Keep up the physical drama and vocal technique while connecting with each person in the room. Stories should be a bit more dramatic than your regular delivery style. Be larger with gestures, movement, and so on, and don't be afraid to act a little bit. Eye contact can also be used strategically when you know the story cold. Effective storytellers help us see and be in the moment with the story. Use your body language to really get across what the story is.

SalesPEAK Secret: Stories should be a bit more dramatic than your regular delivery style.

Expose Your Nakedness and Invite Customers to Become Naked *with* You

When we open a vulnerable spot, "Boy I really messed up when . . . ," we make the situation safe for our customers to expose needs or concerns they might not have shared before, thus giving you new opportunities. The types of stories that might be useful for this are: an embarrassing situation and how you recovered, mistakes and what you learned from them, and misconceptions or assumptions that got you in trouble. Whichever of these you use, remember that they all have two common goals.

1. They lead the customer's thinking in your direction.
2. They help make you look more human and accessible.

Just a bit of caution here: rarely would you want to use a sad story in a selling situation (except in fundraising, which is an entirely separate sales environment). Taking people to a "downer" place is only useful if you show how their action can cure the badness and make the world a joyful place again. Low is not really where you want to go in most selling presentations.

Fit the Story to the Customer's Attention Span—Ninety Seconds—at the Most

The best way to do this is to first, choose a story that is 100 percent yours: it happened to you or in your presence. Next, limit your points to ten key words. Following that, practice your story without words; act it out. Then, when you combine the physical presentation with a limited number of words, you will dramatically improve your customer's reaction to the story *and* get your point across in less time.

A Story's Relationship to the Customer's Circumstances Should Be Obvious

It should be apparent either in the nature of the story itself or in your explanation. A story is like a graph or picture in a presentation; it can:

- Enhance,
- Clarify, or
- Substitute for a complex explanation.

For these reasons the purpose should be clear. A story is only as good as its ability to bring the customer closer to your way of thinking by putting them in a learning situation.

That being said, however, a clever segue will bridge the gap for the customer.

NAKED SALESPERSON STUDY: Richard

A salesperson was presenting a software billing solution to a group of cardiologists:

"Richard was a final-year resident in a busy trauma center. About 3 A.M. the police brought in an older Hispanic woman who was having difficulty breathing. As she gasped for breath, Richard realized that she didn't speak any English. As you all know, he had to assess her symptoms quickly. Two years of college Spanish and six months of volunteering in a migrant worker camp came back to him, and he was able to find out that she had asthma and not congestive heart failure.

"Richard took a lot of courses to prepare him for medical practice—anatomy, microbiology, courses for his specialty in cardiology—and he became a very good doctor. What he didn't take, however, was a class in billing. And, like Richard, you didn't go to med school to deal with collections, receivables, and insurance red tape.

"Our software solution can save you from spending time answering your office manager's questions about insurance issues and other back-office work so that you can do what you enjoy—practice medicine. That's why we are here today. To focus on some easy-to-implement solutions to your practices' billing problems."

No matter how clear you think the story is with regard to the point you need to make, try it out on others before presenting it to a customer. See if your trial listeners immediately get the point or if you have to do a lot of explaining. The immediate "Aha!" is the best kind of story.

> **SalesPEAK Secret:** A story is only as good as its ability to bring the customer closer to your way of thinking by putting them in a learning situation.

The Segue

Sometimes, though, you might have a great story that people like, but don't really see the relevance of. In this case you might still use it, but you will need to smoothly draw the parallel between the elements of the story and the customer's state of affairs.

This is called a segue (pronounced "seg-way" if you've never seen it in print). In music, it refers to a change in the music without a pause, literally "not missing a beat." But for speakers, think of it as smoothing the rough spots of understanding and gluing the story to your product in the mind of the customer. They remember the story; they remember your product; and the message about it resonates when the decision time comes around.

Developing segue skills is an absolute necessity for any salesperson, but it is especially important when using stories or when responding to questions in your presentations.

You never want the customer for even a second to have the thought, "And you're telling me this because . . . ?"

We've talked about transitions, but this is a little more sophisticated. Transitions you build into your presentation to lead your listener from point to point smoothly. A segue, when done well, not only accomplishes a transition but can also lead to a close.

A good segue has the following characteristics:

- Creates a solid and logical path in the listener's mind
- Connects the value and need for the customer
- Demonstrates creative and positive associations
- Never leaves a point hanging

SalesPEAK Secret: A segue, when done well, not only accomplishes a transition but can also lead to a close.

Try It Naked

Here is a little activity to help you develop skill at segueing.

To warm up, have a colleague give you a random word on a piece of paper. Your challenge will be to explain how that word relates to either your product or to a need your customer has. For example: *newspaper*.

You would say:

One of the biggest problems the newspaper industry has is what to do with wasted paper. For your company, the waste is your employees' time while waiting for screens to come up so they can process an order.

Now, you try it on your own. The word is: pavement.

My connection of this to my customer or to my product is:

_____

_____

_____

_____

_____

Before you start rolling your eyes over this seemingly silly exercise, remember that a key to success in sales is the ability to "think on your feet," as the saying goes. Taking an interesting story that gains your customer's attention and turning that attention toward your product is a close in the making. The same goes for questions. Surely, you've heard the term, "spin." All spin does is take whatever has been said and connect it in some way to a positive about a situation or decision.

NAKED SALESPERSON STUDY: Ann-Lin

Ann-Lin, an executive with a marketing firm, got up every day, put on her power suit, and drove her environmentally friendly hybrid car to the ninth-floor parking lot of the largest office building in the city. And every day as she got out of the car, she saw others who were dressed the same as she was, going to the same place she was, with the same look on their faces: boredom. One day, though, as she climbed the stairs with that same group of people she saw every day, she suddenly stopped, turned around, and with a smile on her face, started wrestling her way back down through the herd who looked at her with shock.

Now, depending on what your product is, you can segue to it from any interesting story. If it's a franchise, you would come in at the end, *"and that day she changed her life. She bought a franchise, became her own boss, and now meets a world of interesting people every day as she is making her own fortune her own way."*

Or maybe the point is changing vendors that a customer has used for a long time. *"Though she was happy in her job, she had to wonder if there wasn't something better. You see, we don't always make a change because we're failing or having problems. In business, to survive we have to go after that market opening, or that cost-saving proposal; sometimes we just have to stop to move forward."*

Do you see? Where you started out with your story isn't nearly as important as where you lead the customer back to.

Allowing a questioner to raise a point that might pull the rest of the decision makers away from your proposal can be deadly. You have to be sharp enough to not only effectively field the question but also to segue into a plus for your company—*especially* at the end of the question and answer time. What comes next after Q&A in the presentation is the close, and you definitely want every decision maker in the group thinking your way at that time.

> **SalesPEAK Secret:** You have to be sharp enough to not only effectively field the question but also to segue into a plus for your company—*especially* at the end of the question and answer time.

Sometimes you have to be really creative with the mental connection you build in your segue; other times a customer will ask just the right question, or you'll have just the right statistic to lead from a Q&A to the close. Either way, never leave a story, a question, or even a benefit statement dangling; draw the customer's thinking through a natural progression (the segue) to the next item—the sale.

Using segues is a useful technique for any type of presentation, but you should train yourself to be quick and creative with them. Creativity is often the difference between the information presentation and the sales presentation. Oh, by the way, there is no such thing as an information presentation for a salesperson. Any interaction with a client has an element that supports a close. Webinars and tele-presentations are becoming popular ways to "meet" with customers, since travel costs have gone off the chart. There is no reason to let these be for "information." Specialized techniques will empower you to gain commitments even long distance!

Involved Internet

Yes, we have stressed repeatedly to avoid a dependence on slides. This certainly does not mean that you would always have to speak without slides. Many sales organizations deliver web meetings. For these, the customers are directed to your slide presentation, usually on the company's website, and are guided through it with verbal support, generally on the phone in real time.

If you have ever participated in a dull web presentation, you know it's very tempting to take this time to shop online or play the daily Sudoku. Your customer has the same temptation. But, since this may be your one shot at a long-distance customer, you will have to put on a better show. You do this by involving your client in the presentation, not just flashing a bunch of slides and narrating in a monotone voice. A sales presentation is *not* a documentary on your company's products!

SalesPEAK Secret: Involve your client in the presentation, don't just flash a bunch of slides and narrate in a monotone voice.

Here are some tips to INVOLVE customers in web-plus-slides-plus-teleconferences:

I—*Interest* your customer by preparing something truly creative, something new that may surprise them instead of the usual predictable slide show your competitors have. Work the relationship on the phone using your tone and inflection, then let the slides provide the information that the customers need to see while you are speaking.

N—*Never* be boring! Be especially careful of the ninety-second "eternity" in these situations. (The average person thinks listening to someone for ninety seconds is cruel and unusual punishment.) So if you are reading your slides, it is further torture. Use your customers' names frequently to keep each individual engaged. Ask questions, request affirmation or feedback throughout.

V—*Vocalize* so that your voice is interesting and compelling. If you are on a web camera or videoconference, try to adjust the camera so you can stand. Your voice will sound so much better if you stand and move around. Laugh occasionally, and vary your pitch and inflection as well as the speed of your talking.

O—*Organize* your presentation so that everyone is prepared, especially *you*! Send out an agenda and run a professional sales presentation, not a click-click-click screen show. Remember to use storytelling to make the content more compelling. Plan pertinent questions to engage the customers.

L—*Let* go of preconceived negativity. Some of these online/on-phone sales presentations may have gone badly. That's because they *weren't* naked presentations—they were nonhuman cardboard cutouts instead of connections. Personalize this type of presentation, use specific customer examples, and bring in their comments often. Act like you are having fun—even if you're not!

V—*Vary* your presentation with different types of visuals, maybe even short video clips or snippets of news broadcasts from which you can segue into a plug for your product. Texture the presentation with Q&A and some creative connections between your company's strengths and a prop if you are on a webcam or videoconference. Use a picture of a prop if you have to. Make it memorable! (Remember: if you are not visually creative, ask someone who has those skills to help you come up with clever changeups that are visual. Don't be the "one-trick pony" that can only present in one channel.)

E—*Engage* your customers and encourage participation by pulling in their experiences. Ask them to relate pertinent stories of either your products or of their own business. Use your segue expertise to tie these to the points you want to make. Keep the meeting interesting with an occasional minibreak of humor, but remember to regain control of customers' attention.

Any time you are using slides, you are losing some part of your control over the customer's attention. For web-based sales presentations, videoconferences or the use of slides in a face-to-face group, remember to:

- Develop your own slides whenever possible
- Customize the message for that particular client's situation

- Avoid dark backgrounds for darkened rooms
- Capitalize on the advantage you gain by having fewer and clearer slides

You want to make sure that you are using slides for a particular purpose, and not just using them to use them. If the slides do not serve a real purpose, don't bother.

Humor

Another way to keep attention is the use of humor. This has to be handled in a professional and strategic way—humor in presentations is for a purpose: to sell product, not to entertain.

When we laugh, we remember, the saying goes. Actually, when we have any kind of emotional reaction to an experience or person, we remember. Emotion is processed in the "right brain"; thus, music, color, and feelings of every sort play out in that area. What this means for selling is that your customer will be more engaged and more likely to retain critical decision-making facts if you can create some kind of emotional reaction to go along with the informational message.

> **SalesPEAK** Secret: Humor in presentations is for a purpose: to sell product, not to entertain.

Though you could make them cry, it's generally better to go the other way and use humor to punctuate important points. Humor has many helpful effects, but in sales presentations it is a universal connector.

When you use humor, you:

- Reduce anxiety and stress—improves receptivity to your ideas
- Promote creativity—helps decision makers see how your product can help them
- Enhance remembering—helps recall of all the reasons to buy
- Build a sense of "us"—reduces resistance in the selling situation
- Invoke laughter—makes the customer happy and agreeable

When jokes, customer-relevant cartoons, top-ten lists, and such are sprinkled throughout a site or a stand-alone online presentation, customers are more likely to log on often. But humor should be used with the same strategy as graphics:

- Enhance or clarify the explanation of a customer need
- Solidify the connection between product benefit and customer situation
- Make your points more understandable and memorable
- Respect the sensitivities of all those in the room—don't use anything offensive!

The primary goal of sales presentation humor is not necessarily laughter; it is support for the close. So, if you personally are not particularly funny, it's probably okay because the customers' expectations are for a boring presentation like all the others they've heard. This means it won't be hard to impress them!

> **SalesPEAK** Secret: You may not be as funny off the cuff as you think you are, and many kinds of humor are audience-specific. Tailor humor for your customer.

You need to use what works for you, though. Remember, you may not be as funny off the cuff as you think you are, and many kinds of humor are audience-specific. Tailor humor for your customer. Various formats are available, and some are simple to find or develop.

Cartoons: "Dilbert" cartoons are classic, but there are many others. Can someone in your group develop one just for your products?

Top-ten lists: Give the top ten reasons the (customer's) company is the best in its category (including, of course, the use of your products).

Analogies: "Not using this product is the same as forgetting deodorant before a job interview."

Relevant riddles or word plays: ". . .so when you are wholesaling in the garment business, you want to end up with a clothes close."

Exaggeration: "Your customers will be staying up all night just so they can get to your site at the right moment to buy. Okay, maybe not all night, but . . ."

Photos: Alter them for a humorous effect.

NAKED TIP: In addition to the funny stories and cartoons that you, no doubt, receive in your e-mail each day from friends, many humor items are available on the Internet. For help, go to your favorite search engine and type in "humor" plus the business category of your customer. For example: " humor IT" or "humor Project Management" or "humor stock market." This will help you customize your sales presentation to your client.

A naked salesperson is not a comic, but subtle and occasional humor can be a powerful device for bringing your customer closer to agreeing.

Other tools are available when needed. Following is a brief rundown of the best ways to use each.

A-V APPLICATIONS GUIDE

Type	Group Size	Formality	Interaction
Flip Charts	1–20	Informal	High
Overheads	5–75	Inf./Formal	Low–Med.
PowerPoint	1–500	Inf./Formal	Low
Slides	15–200	Formal	Low
Videos	Varies	Formal	Low
Handouts	1+	Inf./Formal	Low–High
Samples	1–10	Informal	High
Wall Posters	1–50	Inf./Formal	Low–High*

*Posters can be interactive when laminated, and a washable marker is used.

TECHNIQUES FOR OPTIMAL PRESENTING

- Only one visual aid every five minutes.
- Keep the lights *on*!
- Graphics work better than words.
- Use the four-by-four rule with PowerPoint and over-heads: four bullets down and four words per line.
- Avoid reading what's written.
- Don't rely on your visuals to tell your story.
- Check your equipment in advance (lights, timing, connections, etc.).

Nakedness may be a new approach to selling for you, especially in presentations. And anything new is uncomfortable for us—at first. For some of us, even good things take some getting used to. So your own tendency may be to go back to an excessive use of aids, even after you may agree with the suggestions in this book so far.

Aids are just that; they are designed as supports to facilitate a connection with listeners. They can be strategic sales tools or they can detract from your ability to build a two-way conversation and partnership with your customer. If they come away from your presentation remembering clever posters or slides or even videos and *not* committing to your products, you have missed the opportunity.

Whenever you are tempted to overload your presentation with aids of any sort, reread Chapter 1 of this book to remind yourself why you are better Naked.

CONCLUSION

After reading this book and practicing the N-A-K-E-D approach during your sales presentations, you have probably experienced more positive experiences with your customers.

Reflect over the last few pitches you have made. Did you find that:

1. Organizing your presentation was easier?
2. Your delivery was more polished?
3. The content was effectively delivered so that you were more customer-centered?
4. Your decision makers responded more positively?
5. The most difficult questions were handled with more skill and finesse?
6. Your ability to close business was directly influenced by your effective, persuasive, professional presentations?

If you answered "yes" to two or more of the above questions, I can assure you that you are not alone! Thousands of professional salespeople have discovered that by simply using the techniques outlined in this book, they are enjoying more success than ever before.

In Chapter 1, you learned how to avoid overcoming overexposure, by reducing your anxiety before and during your presentation. For example, you learned the importance of connecting and greeting your decision makers the minute they enter the room. There is a two-fold purpose of this approach. The first is to assist you in relaxing by building relationships and putting yourself at ease by making a connection. The second reason is so that the customers can feel that they are there for an important decision and you are part of their influence.

You learned how the greatest speakers, such as John F. Kennedy, Winston Churchill, and Martin Luther King Jr. persuaded from the front of a room and what you can do to emulate their effectiveness in a sales presentation; using passion and *not* an excessive use of slides.

Therefore, after reading and digesting Chapter 1, you gained an understanding of how to:

- Break down the barriers
- Strip away the layers from our buyers
- Achieve mental intimacy with your decision makers

In short, you learned how to get *naked*.

Next, you found out how to effectively and efficiently plan for your sales presentation by beginning with a customer assessment and outlining your goals. For example, you were reminded how important it is to gain a clear understanding of who your decision makers are *before* entering your presentation room. By considering their demographics, their mood, their knowledge of your product, and educational level, your presentation may vary considerably from customer group to customer group.

After conducting your due diligence, you learned how to implement the use of brain bursts to ensure that all of your best ideas were part of your presentation.

In addition, you found out how to open your sales presentation with skill by using an attention-getting approach such as humor, a rhetorical question, a statistic, an outrageous statement, a costume, or other approach that "wakes up" your decision makers before you truly begin.

Lastly, you found out how to link your ideas using transitions and key words. By gaining a clear understanding of how to use your words from the front of the room, a picture can better emerge from your descriptions to solve your customers' most pressing challenges.

While following the steps in Chapter 3, you found out how to keep your customers excited and engaged during your delivery. By communicating your passion and through effective physical preparation prior to presenting, you are now better prepared to deliver in a more professional manner.

You also learned how important it is to have the room set up for maximum persuasion. For example, presenting in a U-shaped table configuration can potentially set up an adversarial presentation situation. By having a clearer understanding of where the key decision makers sit, and how to best connect with them, you discovered the advantages of using oxyproxism to your advantage while presenting.

In addition, by reading Chapter 3, you uncovered the secrets of getting decision makers to read and retain the handouts you so painstakingly prepared in advance. Using color, folders, and fill-in-the-blank documents is a huge plus when attempting to get customers' attention (and keeping it) during your presentations. There is an art to the materials, and you now know those tips.

To provide tips on how to reduce anxiety and to keep your customers involved in your presentations, Chapter 4 provided you with the necessary ideas of how to continue to pull your customers in.

Through a commanding presence and all the tips and techniques professionals use from moving to managing your hands during your presentations, you learned how to manage the room. By using gestures and making eye contact to continue involving decision makers in presentations, you now have the tools to succeed in keeping your customers engaged during your presentation—instead of just leaving it all up to chance.

Lastly, in Chapter 4, you probably gained a better understanding of how to read your customers' nonverbal communication from the front of the room. By interpreting their gestures, eye contact clues, and hand movements, you now know if you are making headway toward a close, or if you need to make adjustments to your presentation on the fly.

Now, everyone knows that the most difficult part of the presentation occurs during Q&A. After reading this book, you can anticipate, prepare and even practice handling difficult questions, however, thinking on your feet while in front of a captive audience can create stress and anxiety in even the most experienced salesperson.

Chapter 5 outlined how to effectively manage just about any type of question or conflict that occurs while you are presenting. Most importantly, you learned how to organize your answers into three parts—providing the information necessary for your customers, all the while, controlling talking too much or too long. True assets for a sales presenter to get to the close!

You also learned how to deflect negativity from your decision makers, to conceal your irritation, and how to handle a heckler or "shooter." By picking up on how to manage the Q&A in professional form, your customers will truly see how you are the salesperson that they most want to conduct business with in the future. Be assured that difficult customer Q&A isn't just targeted at you, but at your competition as well. Our assumption is that they don't have the advanced skills that you are beginning to master and that will show during various presentations.

In Chapter 6, you effectively learned how to get the customers to commit to next steps. Most salespeople end their presentations with a "thank you very much." Pretty dull and ineffective. You are driving the buy by engaging your customers through a commitment along each way of your delivery. As we know, when customers start to say "yes," getting the contract signed becomes simply a formality.

You have uncovered that *the* most important portion of your presentation comes at the end. That's right, just before everyone leaves the room to consider your options and what that means to their business challenge.

As we all know, presenting to those from differing cultures can add another dimension to our sales efforts. Homogenizing a presentation to fit people from all over the world is a daunting task for even the most experienced salespeople.

However, in Chapter 7, we focused on how you can take your presentation and customize it to meet the needs of differing audiences. By appealing to your customers from other countries, you are way ahead of the sales game when presenting your solutions.

You now have resources included that can help you in presenting to specific customers from around the world. We offered some body language, greetings, and protocol that can provide you with a short cut for some countries. However, there may be some homework required from your end, depending on where your decision makers are from.

Lastly, if you are reading this and live in the United States, you were reminded that our everyday vernacular includes many sports expressions and analogies. As a distinctly American approach to conversations, these examples fall flat to people from many other countries. Avoiding the sports analogies is an advantage that will help you think more clearly by using examples that are relevant to your product or service. Again, this is another secret that will help differentiate you from the competition.

Creating color and interest during your presentations is essential to building relationships and keeping your customers' attention while you are presenting. Through the effective use of stories and anecdotes, as outlined in Chapter 8, you are now better prepared to deliver a compelling sales presentation that is interesting to your decision makers.

In addition, you gained a better understanding of how to use A/V in your delivery, without boring anyone with too much of the same thing. By varying your visual, audio, and kinesthetic approaches during your presentation, you are likely to appeal to each individual in your audience.

And how is your passion for your product and service? By taking the quiz in Appendix A, you will uncover how excited you are about what you do, which is essential to your success as a closer.

Now that you have read, used, and digested each page of our book, we invite you to continue to use the techniques while delivering your sales presentations on a daily basis. You're worked hard, so follow the tips, the steps, and the secrets so you, too, can be *the* Naked Salesperson!

Appendix A

PASSION QUOTIENT QUIZ

Circle the letter that best describes the circumstances of your upcoming presentation:

1.	Did you plan and develop the entire presentation yourself?
A.	No, marketing (or some other source) gave it to me.
B.	Yes, I enjoy strategizing and developing what I will say.

2.	When you talk with others about your idea/product/service, how do you feel?
A.	I think what I/we have to offer is reasonable.
B.	Frankly, I can't wait to tell people because this is such a winner.

3.	Thinking of all the obstacles or objections people might have, you:
A.	Like the idea of a challenge because you enjoy winning.
B.	Wonder how the company ever got this far with such a loser product.

4.	Is the phrase "Let's agree to disagree on this one" acceptable to you?	
	A.	That's my signal to rethink and get creative on the spot.
	B.	Somewhat, you just can't sell everyone.

5.	When I have done presentations in the past, I:	
	A.	Generally expect to hit a home run and walk out with an agreement.
	B.	Find that in life you can't expect to win every time; it's a numbers game.

6.	Everyone's together finally, and your slide presentation just won't run at all, you would:	
	A.	Cancel, of course, and reschedule when everything you need is there.
	B.	Use crayons on company stationery if that's what it takes to present right then.

7.	Outside your work do you find yourself to be focused and able to achieve your goals?	
	A.	Absolutely, nothing gets in the way of where I'm going with my life.
	B.	Maybe not written-down goals, but I have a general direction that I'm working toward.

8.	Some people achieve great things; some people end up with truly frustrating lives.	
	A.	Yeah, that last one would be me; I can't seem to get a break.
	B.	Average just isn't going to do it for me; I'm going for more.

9.	How confident are you in the value of the ideas you will be presenting?
A.	This is a revolutionary idea; people just need to hear about it!
B.	It's a good concept, but I'm not sure everyone can see that.

10.	On the way to getting others to buy into your ideas, what do you expect?
A.	Obstacles are bound to spring up, but I'll work around or through them.
B.	If conditions are right, things will go well.

Finally, now rate your own level of passion and zeal about your life and where it's going.

Low   0   1   2   3   4   5   6   7   8   9   10   High

Scoring

The answers below are "P" answers—fewer than eight "P" answers means that you should look at how you really feel about presenting your company's products and services. A low "P" score suggests either a generally low expectation on your part for positive outcomes in general or a low opinion of the possibility of success with your company's offerings.

1: b, **2:** b, **3:** a, **4:** a, **5:** a, **6:** b, **7:** a, **8:** b, **9:** a, **10:** a

Appendix B

POWERFUL
FOLLOW-UP
PROPOSALS

An important aspect to any successful pitch is the follow-up. If you do not follow up on your sales call promptly and professionally, you may lose the buy you worked hard to achieve. To ensure your hard work does not go to waste, follow these guidelines for a powerful follow-up.

TO PREPARE:

1. Have all of your needs assessment questions answered by the customer.
2. Have your ideas clearly thought out and understood so that you can present them in the best light.
3. Be sure the customers' names are spelled correctly.
4. Make sure you know who is to receive copies of the proposal.
5. Use the customer's company colors somewhere in the binder, and as often as possible. (For example, if the customer is the Coca-Cola company, use red binders.)

6. Focus on the customer benefits throughout the proposal (the: "What this means to you is . . .").
7. Give the customer options so that they can make decisions based on variations of *your* company's product offerings.
8. Make the proposal as accessible and interesting as possible. Ideas:

   - Use 12-point font for ease of reading.
   - Use colored paper in a few select places, but don't overdo unless it's for a visual arts type proposal.
   - Use graphics, illustrations, and color—again, don't overdo, but a bar or bullets in blue ink can catch your reader's eye.
   - Include sample materials like software screen captures.
   - Use colored tabs to make it easier to find information.
   - Remember to place headings at the beginning of each section of important information. Decision-makers are skimmers.
   - Put the customer's name on the outside of the binder or folder.

9. Include an "Executive Summary" in your proposal. This is a brief, one-page synopsis that allows the reader to quickly review the purpose of the proposal. *Put this first*, right after the table of contents.

COMPONENTS OF THE PROPOSAL:
- Title Page
- Table of Contents Page
  - Include the page numbers and the major tab headings on this page.
- Executive Summary
- Customer Applications—Situation Analysis or Needs Assessment
  - Don't use the word "Problem" as it's negative and may suggest an insult to the customer.
  - See below for more information.
- Your Company's Capabilities and Solutions
  - See below for more information.
- Completed Project Samples (Here's what the customer will have when done.)
- Product Specifics
  - Use a great amount of detail for technical customers; more "what it can do" for non-tech customers or business decision makers
  - See below for more information.
- Frequently Asked Questions
  - This is where you list the specifics of what the customer is buying. If you include a place to sign, the customer can send this part back to you as a purchase agreement.
- References
- Appendices
  - Here is where you put articles from industry publications about your company or your products; can also include more details of tables or test results here than you had room for in your proposal body.

Customer Applications

In this section, you'll provide the overview of the situation as described by the client. Focus particularly on those items that your customers reacted to during your presentation. Include the emotion behind the customer's problems for which you're supplying a solution. (Example: The President's office is in need of updating so that he can present the company in the best light and indicate a bright future of company prosperity.)

Remember: This is where you remind the customers of the needs that they voiced in your qualifying and paid most attention to during your sales presentation. Use the customer's words from your notes to describe the situation; that way your "insights" into the problem will ring true.

Capabilities and Solutions

This is a good section, but one that salespeople frequently put together poorly in their follow-up. The customer is not interested in your company's entire history, and a generic cut-and-paste from the company's public relations summary or stockholder's report will be seriously ho-hum. Use a razor-sharp editing mind to present *exactly* what the customer will need to solve the problem. Spotlight your company's particular expertise in the area where the customer is concerned. This is also where you will be able to direct the customer to the Appendix, where you have strategically placed a few very positive articles about your company or the product/service the customer will be purchasing.

In addition, be sure to detail what the situation will be like when the product is put into use: "The order processing department will increase order turnaround by 50 percent when our optical character readers are used."

Product Specifics

A thorough yet concise product description will allow your customers to have the details of your product or service at their fingertips. It's important to present your product specifics clearly and directly. You do not want to leave any questions in your customers' minds about what you're selling. Following is a good example of a well put together set of product specifics:

SmartPaper Technology
Gyricon's SmartPaper has similar properties to that of regular paper. In mass production, it is less expensive. Future offices with this technology will be entirely electronic, using several computer screens, a digital camera, no printer, fax or paper.

Electronic paper has been testing for twenty years, with new applications available regularly. The plastic material is flexible and durable. It is an electronically writeable, erasable, and reusable material with endless applications. A major benefit is that information can be changed rapidly.

"Gyricon" means gyrate or rotate in Latin, and that is the concept behind our SmartPaper. Two sheets of plastic are filled with electronic balls that are black on one side and white on the other. When charged by an electronic wand, pen or pencil, the balls spin so that the positively charged color moves to the top. As the device moves, it creates text or images.

This technology can display information on news boards, display signs, or computers via the Internet. The product can be folded numerous times, making it easy to carry. It can be stored in small places. It is the next step in communication material.

This set of product specifics explains the product's function while highlighting its advantages, as well as highlights how the product will help the customer's company.

Remember . . .

Sales presentations work primarily through your customer's listening channel, and that most customers truly internalize less than one-third of what you say to them. Following up with a written proposal will help to ensure that you seal the close.

INDEX

About the Author

Renée Walkup

When she was seven years old, Renée started selling tools and toilets at her family's hardware store in downtown Kansas City, and she has NEVER stopped presenting. In every respect a gifted "salesperson's salesperson," Renée lives what she teaches others. For this reason she has credibility with clients all the way up to the executive level. In 1996, Renée founded SalesPEAK, Inc.® with only ONE prospect. Now years later, a l-o-n-g way from tools and toilets, Renée has sold her way through a client list that looks like a Who's Who of businesses, such as: ING Financial, Pearson Education, BP Solar, USAA, Wells Fargo, The Coca-Cola Company, and dozens of others.

In addition to her expert status as presenter and coach, Renée is considered a telephone selling guru and is also the author of professional development must-read, Selling to Anyone Over the Phone.

About the Author

Sandra McKee

With more than twenty years of experience as an industry presenter, Sandra's speaking background includes corporate training, fundraising for non-profits, sales presentations, speeches at conferences and professional meetings, as well as successful grant proposals in government forums. She has coached hundreds of individuals, among them CEOs, senior managers, salespeople, and entrepreneurs in developing their own speaker's success stories. The Naked Salesperson makes the sixth professional development book for Sandra, whose prior works have sold more than 30,000 copies worldwide. In addition to her writing, speaking, and individual career coaching, Sandra teaches Presentation Skills and Leadership at DeVry University in Atlanta, Georgia.